A Tramp's Philosophy

Bart Kennedy

A Tramp's Philosophy

THE REDISCOVERED CLASSIC OF
Sagacious Twaddle, and Occasional Insight
by One with Erudition
and Experience in Peregrination

INTRODUCTION BY IAN CUTLER

FERAL
HOUSE

TRAMP
· LIT ·
SERIES

Feral House
1240 W Sims Way #124
Port Townsend WA 98368

Designed by Unflown | Jacob Covey

ISBN 978-1-62731-094-9
Printed in the United States of America
10 9 8 7 6 5 4 3 2 1

Tramp climbing on railroad car, date unknown

A hobo "jungle" along riverfront. Saint Louis, Missouri, 1936

Contents

Tramps fighting between railroad cars, date unknown

DESPITE PROLIFIC ADVENTURES ON LAND and sea, the publication of twenty-two books, journal articles and his own weekly magazine, Bart Kennedy (1861–1930) is almost completely unknown today. *Who's Who Online* describes him as having "picked up education in knocking about the world [and that he] drifted into writing." His *New York Times* obituary referred to him as "the tramp novelist ... pioneer of the staccato method of short story writing," and *The* (UK) *Times* obituary characterized his works as "written with vigor, but in a curious jerky style." Never has there been a better time to resurrect *A Tramp's Philosophy*, the first reprinting in over one hundred years, to a new generation, never more addicted to the 'unnatural' world and at a complete loss how to commune with the natural world. The wisdom and humor of this book remain as fresh and relevant today as they must have done at the turn of the previous century, and all the more in need of urgent attention.

A Tramp's Philosophy is more than a treatise on tramping as a philosophy; it is a comprehensive demolition of human civilization in the style of Nietzsche—with whom Kennedy was undoubtedly acquainted—but also the ancient Cynics who drew on lower animals to highlight human stupidity.

And as with Nietzsche, Kennedy applied the term "cynicism" in both its popular negative form as well as in its positive role of denouncing human dogma and stupidity: "It is good to be cynical. It means that the scales have fallen from your eyes." Like Nietzsche, Kennedy both disconnects himself from *and* associates himself with "the masses," using multiple ironies and the form of the diatribe— albeit often softened with mock deference. Kennedy reflects on his ironic and satirical writing style in the final passage of *A Tramp's Philosophy* when he says: "I often say hard things against the world, but even I must admit that it has a sense of humor. Its humor is a humor that has a bite in it, but better this humor than none at all."

Bart Kennedy was born in Leeds of Irish parents, Patrick (a shoemaker) and Catherine. He worked from the age of six in Manchester factories, with no education and nearly illiterate. At around the age of twenty, Kennedy arrived in Liverpool with one shilling in his pocket and began his career as a tramp. He dreamed of sailing ships since he was young, but this was his first sight of them. "You felt that they had come from places a long way off and that they were going to places a long way off. About them was something magical, fine, and strange."

Kennedy was something of a fighter, employing his pugilistic skills at times to subsist as well as survive. His first fight out of England was a few days into the voyage. Incapacitated by seasickness but forced to work his shifts, the regular crew acted brutally towards him, having to take on his share of the work until he became skilled. On one occasion, he fell, and one of the sailors started kicking him. He could hardly stand up at the time but looked the man steadily in the eye and warned him that he shouldn't hit a sick man and that this sick man would get well. Kennedy did get well, crediting the thoughts of getting even with his tormentor as aiding his recovery. Picking his moment when the sleeping quarters were full of sailors, Kennedy got even with his tormentor. He then turned to face the rest of the crew and said quietly, "I'll fight the best man in this watch." There was no response, neither was he bothered for the rest of the trip.

On his arrival in Philadelphia, despite not having a penny in his pocket, Kennedy walked the streets in a state of elation at the prospect of having a whole new world before him. He eventually found himself in the city of Baltimore, where he worked on an oyster boat in the Chesapeake Bay. More fights and near-death experiences followed, including being washed overboard from the schooner in a hurricane and having his yawl surrounded by ice in the Chesapeake Bay. Having grown tired of dredging and concluding that the work was degrading and not fit for a dog, Kennedy resolved to become a tramp. It was after meeting up with an educated, older tramp, Billy, that his real education began. Kennedy's began with a grimy, dog-eared ten-cent dictionary he carried in his pocket, which, with Billy's help, he learned to pronounce "big words" with the correct pronunciation.

Numerous exploits are described by Kennedy in his autobiographical works and all kinds of grueling labor he was forced to take to survive on the way, including an entire chapter in *A Man Adrift* titled 'Shovelling' which Kennedy describes as the most trying and monotonous kind of work there is. As with most of the other tramp writers, Kennedy also spent several spells in prisons on trumped-up vagrancy charges, even though these were often happier times than those spent laboring. In a New Orleans jail, he describes times in good company, with abundant food, and musical entertainment. But there were grim times also, including torture. Kennedy describes the way in which society inside jail mirrored that of the outside world. And it was attending services in a prison chapel—not for religious reasons but as a respite from the otherwise harsher regime—that Kennedy started formulating his philosophy of Jesus, whom he maintains was also a tramp and a criminal while the real criminals in society got off scot-free.

Kennedy would return to sailoring on Lake Ontario and tramping around Toronto before deciding to make the three-thousand-mile trip to the Rockies equipped with a pair of blankets, a drinking cup, biscuits, bacon, coffee, sugar, a .44 caliber revolver with fifty cartridges and a broad sheath knife to protect himself against "Indians and wild animals." It was on this trip that Kennedy formulated his philosophy on the so-called "beauty of nature": working hard in the middle of incredible mountain scenery for months had knocked the poetry out of it. "Neither will fine scenery impress a man when he's hungry, alone, tired, and wondering if he'll get out of it alive." The desolation of being alone in the Rockies affected Kennedy to the point where he describes wrestling with the notion of taking his own life. Several times he put the muzzle of his revolver to his head, but it was while in this most desperate of states that he experienced an epiphany that would sustain him for the rest of his life. "It wasn't fear; it wasn't remorse. I just wanted to live; just wanted to live for no particular reason."

Kennedy would go on to have very agreeable relationships with indigenous Canadians. Tramps rarely hang on to money for long, and when they do come upon it, they get pleasure from sharing it with those without, thereby creating an insurance scheme of survival— and often hard drinking—among the vagabond fraternity. After narrowly escaping being shanghaied, he and his traveling companion Bob then headed off for Departure Bay, where they lived for some time with the Siwash Indians. Kennedy recalls that the hospitality he received with the Siwash was a generosity that outmatched even that of the tramp—an experience that made him question again the "uncivilized" European races, a theme he frequently returns to in this book.

Kennedy did go on the stage for a short spell, but frequent fights with members of the cast lost him his job. Nevertheless, Kennedy stayed in San Francisco for years and had much to say about the agreeable climate and lifestyle he enjoyed in California. Kennedy reasons that after a man becomes a tramp (he never refers to women tramps) and travels from place to place, he gradually develops a philosophy on the subject of work—adding that, given the vastness of America, his reader should not get a false idea that the tramping only involves walking. The tramp is too clever for that, he says; walking would smack of work. So, the tramp takes advantage of the resources of civilization and presses the railway companies into his service. Neither is the tramp particular about the accommodation he occupies on trains, whether this be the cowcatcher of the engine, the front of the blind-baggage, boxcar, bumpers, or even under the carriage lying across the rods. Be this as it may, Kennedy is at pains to point out that true tramps are inherently honest and would rather perish than steal from their fellows. The tramp only resorts to paid labor when he is weak enough; the tramp's true vocation is begging, and he goes to some lengths to emphasize just what a skilled and difficult profession begging is.

In San Francisco, he managed to join another comic-opera company as first bass, singing in such productions as *Der Fledermaus*, *Bocaccio*, *The Beggar Student* and *The Pirates of Penzance*. This company toured the U.S. Pacific coastline, often without making enough to pay the cast their wages, but it was a happy time for Kennedy, and he put his tramping skills to good use for his fellow performers when times were hard. After leaving this company, Kennedy claims that he dined and performed with Sarah Bernhardt for a season at the Baldwin Theatre before taking up an engagement to sing ballads in the Eureka Music Hall on Kearny Street. Following a string of similar engagements, including failing as an actor, Kennedy became weary of the Californian sun and way of life and determined to travel to New York.

On Kennedy's arrival in New York, he took lodgings just off the Bowery, a description of which, in contrast to his eulogy on California, is a delight for the abject and thoughtful characterizations he sketches of that district. By now, Kennedy was beginning to weary of America altogether and returned to Europe.

Kennedy must have started writing soon after this time but had not done with tramping. By this time, he was a man of independent means and could have traveled in relative luxury, yet chose, for the most part, to travel on foot. This included a zig-zag journey from southern Spain taking in most of that country. *A Tramp in Spain* relates his journeys, adventures, and the places he visits, just as any tourist would, but from the standpoint of an experienced tramp. The book opens with Kennedy on board a steamer entering Gibraltar harbor from where he crosses the bay to the Spanish port town of Algeciras. From there, he travels southwest to northeast, taking in Granada, Jaén, Madrid, Guadalajara, Zaragoza, west to Lleida in Cataluña, and then tramps north through the mountains into Andorra and the French border. Kennedy entered Spain with only a revolver, passport, knapsack, and no knowledge of the language, but by the time he reached the French border, he was able to converse tolerably well in the language. Those who wish to read about Kennedy's Spanish adventures, which provide a fascinating account of Spain at that time, should acquire a copy of that text.

In 1897, Kennedy married Isabel Emma Priestly at Holborn, London, the same year that he published his first book, *Darab's Wine Cup*, and when the tramp author was still only thirty-six years of age. The 1911 UK census gives Isabel Kennedy's employment as journalist and editor, although there is no further information as to whether this was in relation to her husband's writing or an independent career. After some time at an address in Reigate, Surrey, the couple moved to an opulent fourteen-room house at 20 Devonshire Place in Brighton. Two years after their marriage, the couple's only child, Rolf Darab Kennedy was born. Kennedy's son, a second lieutenant with 23 Squadron of the Royal Flying Corps, was sadly shot down and killed aged only nineteen, flying a Spad SV11 over the Western Front on 27th March 1918.

The largest part of Kennedy's married life and literary career are unaccounted for in his autobiographical writings. All that is able to be established are the three locations where Kennedy lived between his marriage and his death in 1930. There are the contradictory facts that although he was able to occupy a fourteen-roomed house in one of the most prosperous neighborhoods in Brighton sometime between the dates of 1912 and 1926, he had clearly fallen on hard times. The British Library unearthed information that Kennedy had made several applications to The Royal Literary Fund, established in 1790 for "the provision of grants to writers in distressed circumstances" (the same mission it continues to this day). It appears that after his wife's death, at aged sixty-one in 1927, Kennedy gave up any further interest in life, eventually being taken to the Brighton County Borough Mental Hospital in Haywards Heath, Sussex, in the summer of 1930. A friend found him lying there without food and ambivalent to life or death. Kennedy died on December 6, 1930, at the age of sixty-nine. There is an interesting obituary on Kennedy from the *Ottawa Citizen* dated December 10th, 1930, which states: "Bart Kennedy had a curiously mixed career. Probably it would best be described as built upon sand. But in any event, Kennedy obviously enjoyed every minute of it until two years ago, when his wife died."

Napa Valley, California. More than twenty-five years a bindle-stiff, 1938

"Man is more of a man in the social state that is called savage and uncivilized. Civilization is but a vast, theatric, backward step in the social life of humanity."

—BART KENNEDY
"Cynicisms"

Bart Kennedy
On Society and Crime

Policeman, police dog chasing tramp, New York City, 1912

1

An Odd Gallery.

THERE ARE ALL KINDS of snobs. There is the snob who will snob around a titled person. There is the snob who will snob around a person of wealth. There is the snob who will snob around a great artist, or a distinguished man of action.

It must not be thought that snobs are always people who have a false sense of values. If you are a stout tenor who can shout out a top C in the opera at Covent Garden[1], you will find people who will be extremely deferential to you because of your top C. If you are a poet, you will find people who are only too delighted for you to be rude to them.

The snob lives on snubs. A snub quickens and livens up a snob. For a snub proves to him that you are really what he thinks you are: a high and mighty on-the-top kind of person. You must never by

---

1 Covent Garden is a district in London, on the eastern fringes of the West End, between St Martin's Lane and Drury Lane. It is associated with the former fruit-and-vegetable market in the central square, now a popular shopping and tourist site, and with the Royal Opera House, which itself may be referred to as "Covent Garden."

chance make the mistake of treating the snob as a person on an equal footing with yourself. If you do, you are lost.

Distant, careless notice, tempered with snubs, is the food on which he thrives. And never forget to be rude to him even when you are accepting his homage. I don't mean that you should be rude to him in a barbarous way. Be rude to him in a polite way. However, it is better to be rude to him in any way than not to be rude at all. Still, I would recommend polite rudeness. And if your early training has been such that polite rudeness is not in your anatomy, I would strongly advise you to go and take lessons in the art form from a peer who has inherited his peerage. Such a peer may not know enough to come in out of the wet when it rains, but you will find him a past master in the art of polite rudeness.

Let no one think that the snob is not a useful person. Let no one think that the great and the successful can do without him. But for the snob the great and the successful would perish from the face of the earth. For the great and the successful thrive on the manna of praise and deference even as the snob thrives upon snubs. A great man will sometimes tell you how awful it is to listen to praise. He will tell you how tired it makes him. He will dilate upon the fine time that a mere nobody has when compared with the time that he—a great and well-known man has. He will sigh for the old days when people did not know of his greatness. He will tell you this, but my advice to you is to listen sympathetically to his statement and at the same time to accept it with inward reserve. For the great and distinguished person is talking through his hat.

One of the uses a snob serves is that of a barometer. He is the register of your success—you, the distinguished person. When he comes around, you will know that you have scored a bull's-eye. He will never by any accident come round if you miss the target. So, when you see him, brace up and gratefully wipe your boots upon him. For his advent upon the scene means that you have won in the struggle.

A snob is a disinterested person. For the snob does not want to be great himself. He has no desire to wrest the tiara from your distinguished brow. He does not even wish to bask in your smiles. All he wishes is to be near you. He is well rewarded if you throw him a bone—I mean a look—now and then. For this look he will reward you with shovelfuls of admiration. You say you don't want his admiration? Oh, but you soon will. It is astonishing how quickly great and distinguished persons get used to shovelfuls of admiration. Indeed, the time will come when even the snob will be unable to pile the shovel high enough for you. Be rude to him, of course, but don't be too rude!

The snob must not be confounded with the slave. For the slave is one who is born with the useful instinct to work for others without thanks.

Usually the slave is sullen, for he naturally feels that working for others without even thanks is not such a great catch after all.

Indeed. The snob feels more above the slave even than does the great and distinguished person. And the snob is never sullen. He is the most cheerful and good-humored flunkey in existence.

Though you would hardly think it, the snob is in a way a good sort. If you, the person who is great and distinguished, need money—and you manage it with care—the snob will come gallantly to your help. He will be only too eager to do so. For you are his hero. But don't make the mistake of treating him as though he were your equal just because he places his wealth at your disposal. Always wear the air of superiority. In fact, it is all the more necessary for you to be superior after he has lent you his thousands. You must never forget that the reason the snob took to you in the first place was because of this very air of lofty, starry superiority. When you drop this air, you are defrauding him of his due.

I may as well point out here that the snob has not much use for great and distinguished persons who are free and easy in their manners. He likes his heroes to be exclusive. He likes his dukes and earls and lords and geniuses to stand on their dignity. If you would be the snob's ideal you must be careful. You mustn't bow to every Tom, Dick and Harry you see. Lofty, "Vere de Vere"[2] exclusiveness. That's the ticket.

The snob finds it impossible to understand free and easiness in the great and distinguished. And in the end he thinks that there must be a screw loose somewhere. So be careful, ye great and distinguished! Treasure the tip I have given you. Vere de Vere exclusiveness! That's the touch.

I have never been able to understand why snobs are abused. For it is they who stamp the great with the real, genuine hallmark of greatness. The world finds out suddenly that you are great. But you would soon drop out again were it not for your friend, the snob. For he solidifies, so to speak, the edifice of your fame. He sticks to you closer than a brother. He often enough writes books about you. In fact there was once a snob who wrote a book about an Immortal[3] whom he followed around, and this book is by a long odds a better book than any that even the Immortal, himself, wrote.

So think a time or two before you abuse him.

The snob also holds up the dukes and earls and lords in their lofty places. Where would they be but for him? Indeed, I tremble to think of what might happen to dukes and earls and lords were there no snobs. I shudder when I think of it. Why, they might have to take off their coats and earn a living. A thing too awfully awful to think about.

---

2   "Vere de Vere" references Tennyson's poem "Lady Clara Vere de Vere" based on the English aristocratic de Vere family notable for many famous historical figures. From the 1880s to 1920s the phrase "Vere de Vere" was used as a humorous and derogatory descriptor for a stereotypical member of the British "upper class."

3   "Immortal" is a writer whose work lives beyond their lifetime. The phrase is taken from the informal title "les Immortels" bestowed by the Académie française upon its forty members who serve a lifetime appointment and are considered "the guardians of French language."

No, the snob would be too valuable an asset to lose.

For the snob is the prop and the pillar of the great.

So be kind to him, ye great people. Stand upon him, of course.

But be kind!

T HE UNDERSTRAPPER[4] IS ALWAYS MORE the king than the king. There is more of the ring of command in his voice, there is a harder glare in his eye, his gestures are more peremptory. And when he has been an understrapper long enough, he begins to see that if any accident happened to him the place where he understraps would fall. How dreadful it would be were he to die? How would the great firm to which he belongs survive?

And so the understrapper threats himself with great care. Not because of himself, but because of the magnificent firm in which he draws a modest screw[5]. For here let the fact be put forth that the true understrapper has always modest ideas on the question of screw. The delight of being able to understrap is in itself so great that he would be almost satisfied to work for lower wages than the common or garden men over whom he is set.

After he has done his work for the day he goes along through the streets, dreaming. He dreams of the magnificence of everything connected with the great firm where he understraps. He thinks of his master. He thinks how noble and good and kind he is. He is the finest and best master in the world. And what a magnificent house

---

4 "Understrapper" was in common usage in 18th- and 19th-century England. Originally, the word referred to the assistant to the main laborer, the "strapper." It was adopted by the House of Commons and government workers to describe a junior clerk who had a delusional high opinion of his importance. The modern equivalent would be "underling."

5 "Screw" is 19th-century British slang for wages or salary.

he has in London! Sometimes he walks down the street where it is, just to have the pleasure of looking at it. And what a beautiful house his master has in the country! He has never seen the house in the country, but he has often heard of it. And his master's yacht! He saw a picture of it once in an illustrated paper. It was simply beautiful.

His master is the most perfect man in the world. He has no fault. Well—well, if he has a fault it is that he is too kind. He is too easy. Sometimes he sees people not doing their work, and he never says a word. Of course he, the understrapper, makes up for his master's easy ways. If he finds anyone not doing the right thing he just gives them what for. It would never do to allow the interests of so kind and fine a man as his master to suffer.

The understrapper possesses one of the most shining and beautiful of human virtues.

Disinterestedness.

He thinks not of himself. He thinks of his master. Of his master's great town house, of his master's great country house, of his master's yacht.

Disinterestedness.

All the grandest and noblest men who have lived in the world have possessed this beautiful quality. And the fact that the understrapper possesses it puts him, in a way, into the best company.

How sad it is when he gets the sack.

I say it with grief, but the fact is that the understrapper is usually selected for his position because he is a sneak. But this he does not see. He thinks he has been selected because of his power and his ability. He thinks also that his master likes him.

Which is a fallacy.

For no master ever really likes the understrapper. He invariably looks upon him as a necessary evil. In governing there is a good deal of dirty work to be done, and someone must do it.

Besides, the understrapper is often a nuisance to the head of the firm.

His zeal is too apt to outrun his discretion.

For he takes a narrow view of the relation that his firm has to things and to men who are outside it. He quite often thinks that nothing matters but the firm. If there were no firm, there would be no world, so to speak.

And so it is that he quite often, by his style and manner, offends people who would be of use to his firm. For he does not realize that there are people outside who care not a rap for either his firm or his master. I mean that they do not care enough to take impudence.

And the understrapper occasionally spoils business. I, personally, have known of such instances. I have known when the master had to take hold to try and undo the mischief done by his subordinate.

For there are times when it does not do to be more the king than the king. There are times when it is politic to remember that there are interests outside the interests one is actually engaged in. There are also times when it is absolutely necessary to remember that no firm nor man nor thing is big enough or great enough to stand absolutely alone.

But the understrapper has rarely intelligence enough to see this. However, as I suggested above, he has usually been selected for his post for a reason other than that of intelligence.

I would like to tell the owners of big business that there is no more dangerous man for them than a certain kind of understrapper. I mean the absolutely devoted and loyal and boot-licking variety. Every man is a human being, and I can quite understand an employer in time getting used to people who abase themselves before him. You are the head of a big firm, and your chest naturally swells a bit when you think of it. Here are all these men working for you—thousands of them. You have but to raise your finger, and the best of them would have to go packing. I can quite understand a big employer of labor feeling in the end like a sort of tin god on wheels.

But this is a dangerous feeling for you to have, my good employer, and it is dangerous for you to get used to the boot-licking understrapper.

I know that in your heart you never really like him, but the danger comes when you are apt to put him into a responsible position because you feel he is trustworthy. You are right. He is trustworthy. But he is also a fool.

And never, never put him into a place where anything vital to the interests of your firm may hang upon his judgment.

For the very fact that he is your boot-licker shows that he is a man of no capacity. Men of capacity are never boot-lickers. In the vast majority of cases they are bold, upstanding, don't-care-a-rap kind of fellows—something like you were in the beginning. And even though they are not quite as civil and respectful to you, as you think they might be, still their intelligence shows them that it is well for their interests if the firm does well. The man for your money, my good employer, is the capable, don't-care-a-rap kind of fellow. For he takes a broad view of things. And think not only once, but think several times before you get vexed with him. In fact, if you are really wise, you will make a pal of him. And you will find him in the end infinitely more trustworthy than a million understrappers.

I admit that the understrapper has his uses. For as we all know business has its seamy side. And if you were to run your business on the golden-rule plan, you would find yourself in the workhouse in no time.

The understrapper has his uses, but never, never put him into a place where anything important depends upon his judgment.

For he has got none.

Many a firm has been wrecked by an understrapper.

The understrapper is a slave who was born without even a glimmer of the instinct of freedom. He was born into the world a boot-licker.

And the world is not for such as him. For he is always afraid and trembling. He is afraid even when he is trying to get a ring of command into the sound of his voice. He is afraid even when he is being impudent to those to whom he thinks he can afford to be impudent.

No, the world is not for the understrapper. He pays too big a price for what he gets out of it.

The world belongs to quite a different type of man.

ONCE, LONG, LONG AGO, when I was green and innocent, I imagined that confidence was a sure sign of capacity. The egotistical person who knew it all, and who felt that he could do it all, took me in. I used to listen with respect and reverence to this person's long and glowing descriptions of the powers that lay hidden within him.

In a word, I was taken in by the incapable egotist.

But this was long ago. I have since learned that a man may be as dull and as flat as ditch water and at the same time possess the confidence of Alexander.

I have also learned that real capacity goes with a kind of silence. I mean silence as far as the outlining of what may be done. For capacity in itself means the power of dealing effectively with unforeseen issues. And this is why the man of real capacity has little to say as to what will be the result of his effort. He feels instinctively that his power must lie in the mastering of things and issues that come up unexpectedly.

One of the things that astonishes me in this wise old world is the way that it takes incapable egotists at their own valuation. I respect the wisdom of the world in a great many ways, for the world is old. The world has forgotten more than any of us have ever learned, and I am all the more astonished that it should make this mistake.

Many are the enterprises that have been ruined through the fact that some pushful incapable has been taken at his face value. And here let me state that the pushful incapable need not necessarily be a loud-voiced bouncer. He may be a low-voiced, suave, artistic putter-forth of the powers and qualities he does not possess. He may even assume the garb of modesty. And here let me warn people who have money to put into enterprises to beware especially of the smooth, suave, honey-tongued type of incapable egotist. He is the worst of all. He is the one whose soothing and silken words will be able to make you feel how great and grand and noble you are. He is tact itself. Watch him.

I am not saying that the incapable egotist is dishonest. I do not say that he purposely sinks the ship that the owner has been ill-advised enough to allow him to captain. Indeed it would be better were he dishonest. The dishonest person usually has sense enough not to kill the goose that lays the golden eggs.

No, the incapable egotist is simply a person who is entranced with visions of the glorious things that he feels he has it in him to accomplish. He possesses the divine gift of imagination. And added to this he is dowered with a strong sense of self-value. And also he possesses the magic gift of words. He could talk the head off a mule. And his real and proper place is the Palace of Sounds—Westminster.

I don't wish it to be thought, however, that I am denying that he has his use. He has. For instance, he is of great use to himself. For one of the things that the world dearly loves is the glowing, spoken word. Possess but this gift and you will attain to a high place in the councils and enterprises of men. You will be allowed to lead nations and projects into morasses and bog-holes. Possess but the persuasive, silken and glowing word and people will follow you to the end of the world. You will persuade the green and innocent capitalist to give you all he has and all that he can borrow. You will lead nations over the edges of precipices.

The glowing magic word of the incapable egoist! Oh, that I possessed it! For then I would not be reduced to the writing of alleged prose for a precarious and parlous living. People would rush to me with their thousands and beg of me to do with it as I willed. Or had I possessed this gift of gifts I would by this time have been at the very least a Cabinet Minister. To possess a curt and abrupt and explosive manner of speech is worse than a misfortune.

It is a calamity.

Nothing outfaces the incapable egoist. No matter into what disaster he has led you, he always turns up smiling. He is dowered with a sublime and infinite faith in his own wisdom. His wisdom is as a shining, far, beautiful star. The world rocks and quakes and is overwhelmed, but the star of his wisdom still shines high and serene. He has lost all your money, he has made you genuinely feel that you were an idiot to have had anything to do with him, he has led your army to destruction, he has destroyed your country. And still his wisdom shines serene above the chaos that has been caused by his bungling.

He was at the head of things, he actually steered the ship on to the rocks. But not his was the fault of the disaster. It was the fault of this, it was the fault of that, it was the fault of the other.

Everything was wrong but his own high and serene wisdom. The rocks had no right to be where they were, the wind had no right to be blowing in the direction it was blowing, the ship had no right to be the ship it was. Every imaginable thing was wrong. Everything but his own high and serene and star-like wisdom.

Oh, ye of little faith! Would that ye could take a lesson in faith from the enduring and profound and all-embracing faith that the incapable egotist has in his own wisdom. His wisdom that shines high and clear and beautiful as a star!

I wonder why it is that the world is so fond of words? I wonder why it is that it places the value it does upon them? I don't mean written words. I mean spoken words.

I wish some profound person would rise and tell me why.

But I suppose no one can really tell the reason why.

And will anyone kindly tell me what useful purpose the incapable egotist serves in the world? Will anyone inform me why he ought not to be distinguished?

But, stop! I withdraw the question. I had no right to ask it.

For it suddenly occurs to me that the incapable egotist is an artist. An artist upon whose work there can be placed no base, utilitarian value. His work is at once useless and interesting.

It may be objected that the interest he causes is usually of the painful variety, but what of that? The most enduring kind of art is the art that arouses sad and painful emotion.

Yes, he is an artist, and I am pleased to be able to record that he is an artist who is well paid. Your incapable egotist never lives in a garret. He performs his useless and interesting work in the midst of good surroundings. And he is paid for his work, even before he does it.

Which is a good thing, for if he had waited until he finished his work there would be no money left to pay him.

IT MUST NOT BE THOUGHT that the traitor is a man with a base, dreadful-looking face and a servile cringing manner.

For such a man as this would never get a chance to betray anything. Even were he a traitor—which would not be probable—he would advertise the fact a mile away. No one would trust him. People would be against him because of his looks—because of himself. He would not be allowed to share the councils of any secret organization. And I need hardly say that no such man would ever get behind the scenes in the running of a government.

The most real and effective traitor would be the one who possessed fine physical gifts and who had strong personal magnetism. If the secrets of the Foreign Offices of the world were laid before us, we would find that this was the case. We would find in the immense majority of cases that those who betrayed the secrets of their country were people you would be apt to like if you met them.

I have not in my mind a certain class of spies. Quite often these men show the signs of their dreadful trade in their faces.

I am referring to traitors. Those who betray the secrets of a cause to the enemies of that cause. They are almost always the people whom no one would suspect. They are people capable of inspiring confidence.

Treachery has always been the most severely punished of any of the human acts that go by the generic name of crimes. And all human beings are at one in considering it a crime.

There are many human acts, specified upon the statute-books of the world as crimes, about which there is a difference of opinion as to whether they are crimes or not. Killing is not a crime in times of war. Neither is theft. Again, there are those who consider that willful deliberate killing may, under certain circumstances, be no crime. And so with other human acts of less moment. There is a difference of opinion as to whether or not they are rightly classified in the statute-books.

But there is absolutely no difference of opinion about treachery. All men abhor it. The men who are called honest, the men who are called criminal. Even those who profit by it, abhor it. Though perhaps it may be pertinent to remark here that did human opinion consider the one who profited by treachery as equal in guilt to the traitor, there would be fewer traitors.

However that is not the point.

The point is that treachery is in the very essence of itself an act that is a crime.

I once knew a man who was a traitor. With others I was with him in a certain venture, and he betrayed us. He was a man whom we all liked. An intelligent man and a brave man and a sympathetic man. When I found out that he had betrayed us, I was more shocked than I have ever been at anything since. It was my first lesson in the complexity and strangeness of human nature.

Yes, I felt that he deserved death. But I liked him so much that I shrank from the idea. And still I felt that death ten times over would not fit for the crime he had committed.

He was a traitor!

And still he was a fine fellow in other respects. But his treachery damned him utterly. In fact his very qualities made the crime all the more black. Had he been a mean-looking man, a man whom one sometimes associates mentally with treachery, I might not have minded so much. But he was a frank, fine, interesting, intellectual-looking man.

Have you ever had for a friend one who always went against you whenever you had a dispute or a quarrel with a third person? You probably have had or have such a friend. You may have done this friend good turns, but still whenever you have a row with anyone you find him arrayed on your antagonist's side. It is not that he is friendly towards your antagonist. It is only that he sees where he is right and you are wrong.

You may realize to yourself that your antagonist has a point of view, but you are provoked to think that your friend should see it so clearly and that he should express himself so sympathetically in its favor. In your heart you would like your friend to be a whole-souled partisan of yours.

You really care little for his judicial analysis of the differences between you and your antagonist. And your friendship for him will most likely wane. Indeed it is apt to die out altogether.

In a word your friend has what politicians call the cross-bench mind. He sees both sides of the question, and he is moved towards neither.

A man with the cross-bench mind may seem a far cry from a man who is a traitor, but I am sure that both of them have in this respect the same mental quality. I am sure that the genuinely treacherous type of mind is a mind that really is able to see both sides of the question.

One of a traitor's mental qualifications will be power of cold, clear, judicial vision. And added to this an utter disregard of all interests save his own. A traitor will be a person of strong mentality. And a traitor will also possess courage. For it takes firmness and courage to take the chance of the punishment that may fall upon him. A man who betrays the secrets of an organization, whose object it is to overthrow a government, knows that a terrible price may be exacted from him at any moment for his treachery. He knows also that even the government, in whose interests he has betrayed his friends, will have no sympathy for him should he be destroyed. A man who tells the secrets of his country's defense to an enemy, or a possible enemy, knows that, if he be found out, his country will execute a vengeance upon him that is of the two even more terrible than the vengeance that is exacted from the one who betrays a revolutionary organization.

Over the traitor a sword is forever hanging. And the one who braves this sword cannot be one who is a coward.

A traitor undoubtedly must possess courage. He undoubtedly must possess mental gifts—acumen, sense of balance, observation, coolness.

He must possess magnetism. It is this quality that will be the key that he will use to enter into the confidences of those whom he would betray. He will be supple and daring and shrewd and alert. He will be suave and self-controlled. A boon-fellow. A jolly companion. A personable human being.

Indeed, it is because of his intelligence and his qualities that his crime is so hideous.

Man recognizes that the traitor is of all human beings the being that is most sinister. In the very beginning man could not have survived but for the making and the keeping of pacts with his fellow man. Therefore treachery is the crime that aims against the very root of man. Man fears it as his prototype feared the great reptiles in the world of the dim, profound past.

Still, I cannot refrain from repeating that, did human opinion consider the one who profited by another's treachery, as equal in guilt to the traitor, there would be fewer traitors.

In fact, I will go farther and say that it is as other things in our life. The supply rises to meet the demand.

He who employs the traitor is the greater traitor.

WHAT CAPITAL REALLY IS I HAVE never been able to find out. And the more I think of it the more puzzled I get.

People have often tried to explain the mystery of capital to me. My dull head has never been able to grasp the explanation. And once I endeavored with heroism to read a famous book that told all about it. But I regret to say that my attempt upon the famous book resulted in a headache.

I understand well enough what labor is. For I have had to do it. Indeed, it requires no intellectual giant to grasp the meaning of labor. It is a plain, straightforward, back-breaking proposition that is as plain as a pikestaff to the biggest numskull. You don't require a University education to get the thorough hang of it.

The capitalist—or person who owns capital—is, if anything, a bigger mystery than capital. But for him hundreds and thousands, and, I might say, millions of men would not be allowed the privilege of working. But for the capitalist we would not be able to live. It isn't exactly that he feeds us. It isn't exactly that he gives us something for nothing. But for all that we would be in the cart[6]—if I may use

---

6 "Be in the cart" is a British idiom with origins in 16th-century horse racing. The phrase originally meant that a worker prevented the owner's horse from winning a race. The idiom reached peak usage in the late 19th and early 20th centuries as the British colonial forces used the phrase to describe any situation that jeopardizes the success of one's "betters," in both military and civilian scenarios.

a slangism—but for the capitalist. Why we would be in the cart, I don't know. But it is certain that we would be in it.

And here let me express my humble thanks to the capitalist for allowing so many of us to live. I don't properly understand what he does, or how he does it, but I am very much obliged to him for all that.

The capitalist is a mysterious being who does everything and at the same time does nothing. Compared with him the genie of old was a very simple person indeed. The genie did astonishing things because of the power that was in him. But the capitalist is no more than you or I or the next man. And still he is as powerful as the best genie you ever heard of. The capitalist may be taking it easy in his club and still at the same time be performing some gigantic engineering operation in a distant part of the world. He may be in Paris and at the same time he may be building a Suez Canal. He may be in London and at the same time he may be building a battleship.

The whole thing is wonderful. The modern capitalist beats the ancient genie into a cocked hat. He at once does nothing and everything.

And more wonderful to relate still, he does everything with absolutely nothing. Or at any rate with what appears to be absolutely nothing.

For our capitalist doesn't even pass the gold that is alleged to represent capital. He just puts his name on a bit of paper, and lo! the thing is done.

Mind you, I don't say that capital is nothing. I only say that I cannot for the life of me understand what it is. I know, of course, that there are many wise persons who understand it thoroughly. But, I repeat, I don't understand it. To me it is the biggest of big mysteries.

But I don't want to put myself down as being altogether a fool. For instance I can understand how it was that Napoleon was so great a conqueror. It was because he had a genius for generalship. And because he had an army—and led it. I can understand why Caesar conquered the world. He was actually there at the conquering. But how a man can at once build a big battleship, and at the same time never even see it, is a mystery too deep for my intelligence to grasp.

And the explanations given only, as I said before, puzzle me more. For the explanations, when pinned down, amount to this: You see a man, or perhaps you don't see him or even know him. And he may even not know you. And he does something. And only for you—who may not even know him—he could never have done this something.

I tell you this is wonderful. And it is happening all the time in our modern life.

Miracles! Why, the miracles told of in the Bible are as nothing when compared with the miracles a capitalist performs.

When I think of the capitalist I am filled with the utmost admiration and reverence. And this reverence and admiration is only heightened the more by my being utterly unable to understand how he works his miracles. And I may say that it is heightened even still more by my utter inability to grasp even the detailed explanations of the workings of his miracles.

There is another wonderful thing about the capitalist. The capitalist may be an infant in arms, or a weaker-minded person than usual, and still he is able to perform the above-mentioned miracles. All that is necessary is to get deputies to sign the bits of paper for him.

There are, I may say, in this world churlish people who are always grumbling about capitalists. There are wrong-headed, unthankful people who have the assurance to assert that capitalists are the enemies of the human race. But the world has never yet been free of soured, grumbling cynics.

These same grumbling cynics are a danger to us. For if they persist in girding at the capitalist, why, the capitalist might get the huff and depart with his capital. And then what would become of us? What would happen to England if all the capitalists departed? How would we get a living? How would I get a living?

True, it might be said by the shallow person that if the capitalist flew off with his capital he would still leave the land, and the power of the land to grow food, and the laboring person who tilled the land, and the men who made battleships, and even the men who would fight to save England from disaster.

I know quite well that if a great capitalist were to go off from us the sun would still shine, or not shine, on dear old England in the same old, time-honored way. I know quite well that on the surface it looks as if the capitalist might not matter. Dogs would still bark, people would still live and die, the seasons would still come and go.

It looks as if it would be the same, I admit. And still it would not be the same at all. Why it would not be the same I can no more tell you than the man in the moon. All that I know is that it would not be the same.

This being the case, I am very much against these people who abuse the capitalist. To fall out with your bread and cheese is silly. The capitalist gives us our bread and cheese. How he gives it to us I— Well, I don't want to repeat myself too much. But he does.

And my counsel to the sour cynics is to let up. Be like I am. Be polite. Don't irritate the capitalist. If it is possible that you are as stupid as I am as to how he manages to do things without doing them, why, say nothing—or, if you must say something, let it be by the way of expressing your humble reverence and admiration. Express your humble thanks to the capitalist for allowing you to live. Salute him humbly, as I salute him.

And think of the awful fate that would befall the world did he not exist!

CROOK IS AMERICAN SLANG for habitual criminal—one who is crooked or twisted in character, who loves the devious path, who couldn't run straight whatever happened. A crook would sooner make hundreds a year by shady practices, than thousands by honest and noble and ideal methods. Were you ever to give a crook a Prime Minister's job he would still manage to do something or another that would lodge, or ought to lodge, him in jail.

Not all crooks show their characters in their faces. I mean they don't show them to the ordinary eye. For a crook may be a distinguished-looking man with a noble brow and a straight, honest eye. You would be astonished at the fineness of appearance displayed by some crooks.

According to the learned Lombroso[7], who measures up human beings exactly and mathematically, a crook is a degenerate. There is something lowering in his glance, etc.

He is wrong. I would wager that many a bishop is a crook. And, as everyone knows, all lawyers must be crooks.

Let it not be thought that crooks are people who are vicious and maleficent of character. Let it not be thought that they are people who have a spite against humanity. For such is not the case.

The crook is generally a person with a sense of humor, and no man can be wholly lost who possesses this most divine of all the senses. Lawyers are the most delightful fellows to meet in the world. For they are so used to seeing that black is white and white is black

---

7   Cesare Lombroso (November 6, 1835 – October 19, 1909) was an Italian criminologist, physician, and founder of the Italian School of Positivist Criminology. Lombroso rejected the established classical school, which held that crime was a characteristic trait of human nature. Instead, using concepts drawn from physiognomy, degeneration theory, psychiatry and Social Darwinism, Lombroso's theory of anthropological criminology essentially stated that criminality was inherited, and that someone "born criminal" could be identified by physical (congenital) defects, which confirmed a criminal as savage or atavistic. Lombroso's research methods were clinical and descriptive, with precise details of skull dimension and other measurements. Although he gave some recognition in his later years to psychological and sociological factors in the etiology of crime, he remained convinced of, and identified with, criminal anthropometry. After he died, his skull and brain were measured according to his own theories by a colleague as he requested in his will; his head was preserved in a jar and is still displayed with his collection at the Museum of Psychiatry and Criminology in Turin.

that the foolishness of hard and fast definitions becomes apparent to them. They realize that truth is the most elastic and twistable thing going. And so it is that they are men who are able to laugh. I must confess that I like lawyers.

The crook is an artist at the game of life. He likes deviousness for its own sake. The straight path he abhors. He would sooner wander through bypaths and shady places than go along broad, sunlit roads. He would far rather do you out of a hundred pounds by the exercise of his wits than receive from you a free gift of a thousand. He likes to make human beings do things without their knowing that he is making them do them.

In fact, he is a decent fellow who often goes to jail. That is if he belongs to a certain class. If he is a lord or a bishop the world quite often treats his crookedness as if it were eccentricity and aberration. And the world invents words to replace the rude and vulgar terms that are ordinarily used to characterize the doings of the crooks of the lower classes.

And here I am sure that everyone will agree with me in what I am going to say—at least everyone will agree with me who has to do with governing.

It is not the crooks who give the most bother to Society. Rather is it the good and disinterested people who possess the idea of running the world. It is they who give the most trouble to the guardians of law and order. Not the thieves and professional criminals. Oh, no. The police have at heart kindly and brotherly feelings towards them. The crooks are really the employers of the police and judges. Ideal employers.

Philosophers, who have no sense of humor, are fond of saying that humanity is only too eager to have the world run on fair and straight lines. And these unhumorous philosophers blame governments because the world avoids the copy-book maxim as it would the plague. The real truth of the matter is that responsible, governing men follow public opinion slavishly. And they know through sad experience that humanity is composed of innumerable persons who are all out for the success of their own hands. When a man gets to be in power he sees a thing or two that he never saw when he was in opposition. And note this: You never hear growls and grumbles but from people who are not in power. Put idealists and lofty-browed people into office and they at once become as quiet as mice. The world at heart loves the line that is devious and crooked.

The crook is simply the expression of the world's inherent crookedness. And the reason he is not dangerous is because he is really in consonance with the ideal of the world.

Why he is punished at all, I don't know. Though to be quite fair one must admit that it is only a small section of his class that is punished. The world is not such a big hypocrite after all. Indeed to the majority of the crooks it acts in the fairest way it can. See how decently it treats an empire builder.

No, the world is fairer than the cynic makes out.

Westminster Abbey is full of crooks.

And I must say that it makes me tired when I think of the way that the world has been insulted, and is being insulted, by the irresponsible ruffians who are called men of genius. The world is called unfair and hypocritical and horrible by these people. When all the time the world acts as straight—or, I beg pardon for the slip—acts as crooked as it can.

Men of genius ought to be locked up.

Mr. Lombroso suggests that the crook is an atavism—a throwback to the men of primal times. And out of his suggestion comes the inference that the world only locks him up because the world wishes to advance upon different roads of progress.

It may be that the crook is an atavism. But the inference that the world locks him up because it would like to travel now on different lines is all wrong. The fact is that the world only locks him up when he is guilty of small, twopenny-ha'penny[8] methods. The world likes the crook to work in big and noble strokes. It likes his effects to be broad and sweeping and commanding.

Take Napoleon—the biggest crook the world has known. See what the world thinks of him.

The truth of the matter is that human nature is now as it was in the days when it lived in the cave. It has exactly the same ideals. Ten or twenty thousand years in the life of man is not as significant a lapse of time—as far as the changing of human nature is concerned—as some idealistic gentlemen would have us suppose.

Take revolutions. They are simply wrangles as to who will collar the swag. The crooks who are out want to get in.

Man himself is the prime and chief crook of the whole animal kingdom.

But for all that I am not going to have him libeled. I am not going to have it said that he is really down on the crook. I am not going to have it said that whilst he is a crook himself he has the hypocrisy to punish crooks who don't crook according to certain rules.

For he is not really down on crooks at all. He is at one with them.

But he would like them to have larger ideas. He would like them to spread themselves more.

And it must in fairness be said that in the main he is not even down upon the crooks of the small, twopenny-ha'penny methods if they take the precaution of being rich, and well placed in Society.

8　"Twopenny-ha'penny" is a variant of "Tuppenny-ha'penny." The phrase specifically means "two pennies and half pennies" and is 19th-century British slang for something cheap, tatty, and tawdry.

T HE JUDGE INVARIABLY POSSESSES a rare gift of humor.

The laws that govern human nature are too deep for anyone to understand, and it may possibly be that when a man is raised to the dignity of judge there is bestowed upon him in some mysterious way this fine gift.

Even the immortal Leno[9] could not have raised a laugh more quickly than one of these grave, bewigged, solemn men. And stage comedians might do far worse than to go to court and take lessons from them in the laugh-making and smile-creating art. They would learn that secret of secrets of all art—that the best effects are got in the simplest way.

Of course, like other human beings, judges have hard critics, but I am pleased and proud to say that I am not one of them. I have too much respect for the Bench to be at one with certain ruffians of the Press who have the impudence to suggest that sometimes the humor of a judge is of a feeble character. Why such calumnies are allowed to get into type passes my comprehension. Why such ruffians are not put into jail also passes me. Seriously, there is altogether too much license allowed to people like this.

Once I was sued by a trades-person for an alleged debt. Well do I remember the time. I stood on the judge's left, while the trades-person stood on his right. The trades-person and I argued the matter out, while the judge threw now and then between us an illuminating word. He, the judge, was a weary, dignified-looking man with a deep voice.

---

9   Dan Leno (birth name: George Wild Galvin), December 20, 1860 – October 31, 1904, was a leading English music hall comedian and musical theatre actor during the late Victorian era. He was best known, aside from his music hall act, for his female roles in the annual Christmastime pantomimes that were popular at London's Theatre Royal, from 1888 to 1904.

The argument was going briskly on, when suddenly the judge made a remark. It was a simple and homely remark. There was nothing brilliant or intellectual about it, and to an undiscriminating ear it might seem as though it were about nothing in particular. But still there was in it a subtle, pervasive something. It was a simple remark girded round with a something. What that something was I am now unable to tell. But it made me roar with laughter. I tried to catch the judge's eye as I laughed, but he was too good an artist to let me do that.

And I roared again. The judge's humor was of such a deep and penetrating kind. It caught and swept me away. His remarks on the surface appeared to be neither wise nor witty, but deep down in the heart of them there was the subtle, evasive, laughter-evoking quality.

I have often tried to analyze this wonderful and glad talent that blossoms in the dull atmosphere of the court. For there is in the main a key to every mystery. And I have come to the conclusion that it is not so much the remark that the judge makes as the way he makes it. In a word, the secret is in the style. It is in the way that the utterance is clothed as it issues from the lips of the grave and august person who sits upon the bench. The wittiest remark falls flat if uttered in a certain manner.

I tremble to think of what might happen did the judge make a remark that outside, carping persons would account as really brilliant. The people in court would certainly explode. It seems to me that I have at last hit upon the reason why judges make remarks that are apparently trivial and commonplace. Their style of delivery of a joke is so perfect that the joke itself must be, so to speak, of a slight kind, so as not to create too loud and uproarious a laughter. The feeling of the true artist makes them tender and considerate of their audience.

Besides possessing a rare gift of humor the judge also possesses a profound gift of wisdom. Here again I am forced to speak chidingly to those obtuse and vulgar persons who now and then dare to raise their heads and proclaim that on rare occasions a judge is not so wise as he might be. I must, however, do these persons the justice to say that it is only occasionally that they question a judge's wisdom. The humor of a judge is by comparison questioned fairly often. But his wisdom is only questioned rarely. And here I must pay a tribute to the English character. It has its faults, but the non-recognition of a fact is not one of them. When an Englishman sees a person in a high place he realizes at once that he is there. He wastes no time bothering himself as to how he got there. He is there, and that is enough. So when he sees a judge sitting on the bench he knows that he must be a person of the wisest order to have got there.

But, alas, malcontents are always with us, and it is to the malcontents I speak. They don't count in this instance, of course, but I cannot deny myself the pleasure of giving them a dressing down.

Occasionally, I will admit there are times when a judge does not appear to be the Solomon that he really is. I myself have now and then heard judges say things that made me wonder if I were awake. But there is a reason for everything, and the reason of this apparent lapse is because judges are guided, on rare occasions, by a wisdom that is even more wise and profound than their own.

They are guided by Law.

I must explain that Law is the concentrated essence of the wisdom of all the judges that have ever existed. To use a somewhat vulgar simile, it is boiled down in a handy manner into the shape of books. Perhaps handy is hardly the word I should have used—for these books are great in number and large in size—but it is only the word that occurs to me at the moment.

It is on the rare occasions when the judge refers to this concentrated wisdom that the mistake arises as to his own individual wisdom. But this is neither the fault of the judge nor the fault of the concentrated wisdom that he has evoked. It is the fault of the shallow carper, who is unable to pierce beneath the surface of things. For it is well to put forth the fact here that it is as difficult for the common or garden mind to grasp the wisdom of the Law as it would be for a bushman to grasp the problems of Euclid.

The Law is a thing far above the reach of the common, ordinary human intellect.

But who is the one who dares to question it? For is it not the wisdom of the wisest boiled down?

Even the fairness of judges has been called into question, but this matter I refuse to go into. There are things that are too sacred for the mind to dwell upon. I can only say that the people who do this will surely meet their just reward in another and not a better world.

I am glad that I am not of these people. They are utterly depraved and lost to all sense of reverence and respect. Why they are allowed to exist at all is astonishing. But this world is filled with mystery.

I am proud to say that a judge can afford to look from his lofty position and smile judicially upon these carpers who question his wit and wisdom and fairness. He is there on the bench, and there he stays. He sits, a profoundly deep and sacred and learned person.

And I hope he won't object to my humble self acting as his advocate. And I also hope that if ever I have the felicity to gaze at him fully from the dock he will remember that in palmier[10] days I defended him.

I LIKE THE "CORNER BOY." He is a delightful philosophic loafer, and he is always civil. He is always ready to give you the fullest information concerning streets in the immediate neighborhood.

---

10   "Palmier": an adjective also rendered as "palmy" and commonly used in 18th-century England to describe something as prosperous or flourishing. Rarely used today.

His natural ease and charm of manner might well be copied with advantage by the person whose ambition it is to shine in Society. The busy rusher after the money belonging to other people has of necessity a manner that is abrupt and wolfish. And after the busy rusher has purloined a plenitude of money—through the hollow pretense of business—I can well understand his ambition to acquire a ducal ease and repose.

For let me tell you, my dearest reader, that manners are of more real import than money. That is as far as people other than yourself are concerned. Manners are a sympathetic and beautiful currency that never fails the possessor of them. Should you possess good manners your pocket—if I may use so vulgar a simile—is never exhausted.

The corner boy has perfect manners. He has had the time and the leisure to perfect them. And, were such a thing possible, I would have him as a tutor to the hurried, anxious-faced, business pirates who are searching after "Vere de Vere" repose in their declining years.

And here my dear reader I must correct an impression that it is quite possible you may have. It is quite possible that you may in your mind confuse a corner boy with a hooligan.

Don't do it. Don't do it, my reader. For I assure you that a hooligan and a corner boy are not even distantly related. A hooligan is a violent, strenuous, unmannerly person who quite often will assault you and steal from you without conforming to the rules that govern stealing. A hooligan is even more impolite than a businessman who is getting rich quick. For the businessman conducts his thievery according to certain rules. But the hooligan will rob you without any rule at all. The hooligan is a dreadful person. And wide though my sympathies are, I am obliged to confess that he is excluded from them. You can understand, therefore, the pain it gives me when I find people confusing my dear friend the corner boy with the hooligan—this first cousin to the Paris Apache.

The corner boy usually chews a straw. That is, he chews a straw when he has evolved to the very highest notch of himself. The chewing of a straw is a sign that the corner boy has reached the acme of ease and cultivation.

Why he chews a straw I don't know.

But I do know that the chewing of a straw is a sign that he is all right.

There are cynical people who say that the reason a corner boy is so polite to the inquiring passer-by is because he thinks the passer-by might conceivably stand him a pint as a reward for his information. But the cynic, even at his rosiest, is somewhat of a jaundiced person. He is a person whose delight it is to dwell upon the sere and yellow side of humanity. He is always looking out for the blemish on the skin of the apple.

I am a charitable man, but I must confess that my charity becomes a bit strained when I think of my friend, the cynic. And were he to retire to a different world—I would not mind whether it were better or not—I would scarcely grieve.

The truth of the matter is that the straw-chewing corner boy is polite because he is genuinely sympathetic. Long thought has made him feel a sorrow for humanity. He exists in a world where foolish people are dashing about, doing nothing in particular. He has learned wisdom in the years that he has held up his corner. He has grown to be tolerant, for to know humanity is to become unsevere. And so he answers your questions. And the main reason why he accepts the price of a pint from you is because he does not like to hurt your feelings by refusing.

Dear, gentle, corner-upholding, straw-chewing philosopher! I admire you with the strongest kind of admiration. Your mission in life is to show people that all this rushing after wealth, and what is called honor and glory, is the merest of mere illusions. You watch the world and humanity from the corner of your beloved pub!

Heed not the vulgar persons who have the assurance to say that you ought to go forth and indulge in rude toil! But I know that it is not necessary for me to thus adjure you. The serene wisdom that comes to those who wait is with you. You have learned to stand calm before the assaults of hurrying vulgarians.

Good old corner boy! Long may you quaff the cheap and foaming pint!

THE REVOLUTIONIST IS A RUDE and annoying person who is always grumbling and growling about the powers that be. He has nothing but the hard word for emperors and kings and presidents and capitalists. Should the unfortunate capitalist make a swift million by the sweat of his intellect, up goes a shout of execration from the revolutionist. Should an emperor or a king or a president, or any other ruling person, bring on a little war, there is another shout. Always grumbling. Always growling. I wish the revolutionist would stop it.

For the longer I live the more do I see that the ruling people are the noblest of the noble. They have a large and airy and easy way of doing things. Their scorn of the twopenny-ha'penny method of doing business wins me. My admiration arises when I think of the magnificent way that Andrew Carnegie showers light-giving libraries upon a darksome world. And when I think of the vast sums that American millionaires pay for the works of old masters, a longing to lay down my trusty pen seizes me. I would like to be able to pick up the artistic brush and join the multitudes of jolly artists who are, at this present moment, earning a steady and safe living by the production of the works of the revered old masters for the American market. But alas, my desire is an idle desire. For I cannot paint. But one thing I can do. I can repel herewith the base libel that runs to the effect that the millionaire does not encourage modern art.

This is a digression, however. I must get back to my revolutionist.

Surely, my good revolutionist, you must be aware of the fact that emperors and kings and presidents and Cabinet Ministers and millionaires and Members of Parliament, and even County Councilites, serve a useful purpose! Surely you must know of that dear old scientific wheeze which runs to the effect that there is a place and a use for all things! Listen, my lad. Kings and emperors represent the splendid and pictorial side of humanity. Cabinet Ministers and Members of Parliament represent idealism and self-sacrifice. Millionaires represent—well, millionaires represent the earnings of the lower orders. And as for County Councilites! Well, you have me there. What they represent is too deep for me to fathom. But that they represent something, I'll be bound.

It saddens me to think of the way that revolutionary ruffians impugn the noble motives that prompt the people who do us the honor of doing our little bit of governing for us. They abuse even the police and judges. In fact, they abuse everybody who earns his living by the guiding of humanity along the beauteous path of rectitude. And here with shame must I admit that I myself was once a revolutionist. I used to grumble at the noble and ideal persons whose job it is to guide humanity along the beauteous and luminous path of rectitude. But the privilege of contact with some of these people has shown me how good they really are. For instance, contact with politicians has shown me the inner gold, so to speak, of the politician character. Listening to their sentiments, as they regenerated humanity over cigars and whiskies and sodas, has shown me how wrong I was in the old days when I abused them. It is the same thing with wealthy men. They are nice, kindly fellows who in the main take spacious views of life. I tell you, my good revolutionist, there is nothing like having plenty of people working for you. It makes you easy and assured and strong and gracious and fine. You must try it.

Listen, my dear old friend. In my heart I like you, though you are a grumbler. But the fact of the matter is this: All men, or practically all men, feel that Heaven gave them a mandate to rule and govern their fellows. Show me a man who would be too modest to be a Cabinet minister! You may, of course, have met such a man. But I have never had that happiness. Indeed, my dear boy, I am not quite sure that even you would refuse the job. I know that I would jump at it—I, an old, ex-revolutionist.

And all men desire wealth. Even I could do with a bit. And all men dislike work. I mean they dislike real work. Pick me out a man whose ideal it is to be a navvy[11] or a miner!

Dear, good, old grumbling comrade! Let me tell you that it takes the revolutionary thinker a long time to figure out the truth that the rules of Society are only a reflection of the people who form Society. When he finds out this truth he will likely enough become a jovial and jolly person.

Yes. This world is exactly and absolutely the world that people want!

I HAVE A REGARD FOR THE GIPSIES, because they are people who have intelligence enough not to work. They just wander from place to place, taking life with philosophy and ease. They sleep out under the stars or rain or whatever comes along. People of the open air. Fine, healthy, well-conditioned, philosophic

---

11   "Navvy" is 19th/early 20th-century British slang for a civil engineer employed in navigational canal excavation, then railway building, but later used to describe a general, unskilled laborer, often in construction. Rarely in usage post-World War II, the word had a brief resurgence in 1983.

"Navvies" traveled the world following the work and developed both a distinct culture and rhyming slang. (e.g., "now, Jack, I'm goin' to get a tiddley wink of pig's ear; keep your mince pies on the Billy Gorman." This means the speaker's going for a beer, and asking the person being addressed to keep his eyes on the foreman.)

people. Yes, well-conditioned! For they have plenty of good air to breathe. Which is more than can be said even for the people who dwell in great palaces.

I would like to wander along with them, breathing fine air, doing no useful toil, and occasionally commandeering the nimble and succulent chicken. Commandeering? Well, after all they commandeer very little. The world's real thieves and rogues dwell in magnificent places, and buy titles of honor from governments.

The gipsies are honest and intelligent and healthy. And, moreover, they are a picturesque feature in a rushing, drab, unintelligent and un-picturesque age.

Let 'em alone, you policemen and lawyers, and landlords. Let 'em alone, you rogues. There is more honesty in one gipsy's finger than in the whole pack of you.

Children of a glorious, far, far away past when men wandered about taking life as life should be taken!

Why is there such a growl and a grumble about them because they will not dally with toil? Surely there are enough people who are anxious and eager to work. What about the myriads of unemployed? The world is packed to the brim with hard workers and strikebreakers and other idiots of the thick-skulled order. The world is worried by people who are continually shouting out for the blessing and privilege of toil. The gipsies are coy. Charitable, kind-hearted people who have too much feeling and good nature to rob eager people out of a chance to do hard work.

How I revere this intellectual, clear-eyed, ragged race. These people who wander along carrying their houses with them.

I can well understand landlords grumbling at them. For they do the poor, hard-working landlords out of the rent which is theirs by direct and specific mandate of God.

But I can't understand any unbiased person saying a word against them. That is, if the unbiased person possesses but a rabbit's intellect.

For the gipsies have solved the problem that bears all men to an untimely grave.

The rent problem!

Noble, clear-eyed, and ragged race! Do you really belong to us, the foolish people of this Earth? Or are you of some more intelligent world? Or are you the remnants of some race that lived in this world long, long before the imaginative record, that we call history, began?

Will you tell us the secret of where you get the power of will to refrain from toil? Will you tell us the process by which you harden your hearts against the poor, industrious hard-working, tender-conscienced landlord?

Alas! I fear you are too wise!

Roaming over the whole world. Paying no rent. Doing no work.

Be envious, ye poor, anxious, parlous, miserable rushers after money! Be envious, ye rushers after fame! Be envious, ye foolish intriguers after the worry of the will-o'-the-wisp that is called power. Power is an elusive, fading thing. It faded even from the grasp of that Titan interferer and rusher, Napoleon.

I would far rather be a gipsy than be Napoleon. I would far rather be a gipsy than an anxious-faced money bagger.

A gipsy realizes that the world was given him to enjoy.

For the world is a beautiful place—with its rivers, its winds, its green fields, its noble trees, its fresh clear air, its seas, its ever-changing aspects, its seas, its wide waters. The world is very beautiful indeed when one has eyes. The day is wonderful, and the night is beautiful. The sunlight is beautiful, and beautiful is the light of the far stars.

The gipsy is one who has eyes.

I see them as I tramp here along the road. They stop me and ask me for cigarettes, and sometimes they mistake me for a travelling bank. But what of that? From the worldly point of view it is a tribute—a tribute to my prosperous appearance.

I like to watch them at their fires when they are encamped in their places off from the road. How beautiful these fires shine out as one is going along by night. I often feel that I would like to stop and have a meal with them. A fowl is never so succulent as when it is roasted in the open.

I know it, for I have tried it. And the fowl tastes none the worse for being borrowed.

I remember how delighted I used to feel when I was on the stage, in the old days, singing in the gipsy chorus of "The Bohemian Girl." A lifting, ringing, joyful, thrilling chorus. As I sang in it, I felt all the joy of the wanderer. The great musician, Balfe[12], had caught the whole of the magic and beauty of the gipsy's life in his wonderful chorus. This gipsy chorus in "The Bohemian Girl" is one of the greatest things in music.

Whenever I see the gipsies, as I am going along the road, the sounds of this beautiful chorus come back to me. Again I am on the stage in a country far away from England. I am one of a crowd of gipsies, moving to and fro and passing and repassing upon the stage. Our voices are ringing out, "Where the wolf makes his lair. Where the wolf..." I remember how the basses—of whom I was one—used to come in here. I wonder where the members of that chorus are by this time—the men and the girls! The beautiful stage scene comes up to my mind whenever I see the gipsies here on the road.

These harmless and delightful wanderers. Only a stupid churl would think of interfering with them. For they are one of the few romantic elements that are left to us in this retrogressive age of

---

12 Michael William Balfe (May 15, 1808 – October 20, 1870) was an Irish
    composer, best remembered for his operas, especially *The Bohemian Girl*.
        After a short career as a violinist, Balfe pursued an operatic singing career,
    while he began to compose. In a career spanning more than forty years, he
    composed at least twenty-nine operas, almost 250 songs, several cantatas and
    other works. He was also a noted conductor, directing Italian Opera at Her
    Majesty's Theatre for seven years, among other conducting posts. In 1843,
    Balfe was in London where he produced his most successful work, *The
    Bohemian Girl*, at the Theatre Royal, Drury Lane. The piece ran for over one
    hundred nights, and productions were soon mounted in New York, Dublin,
    Philadelphia, Vienna (in German), Sydney, and throughout Europe and
    elsewhere.

machines. They are an object lesson in a sordid, money-grubbing age. They make one feel that the best-your-neighbor ideal is not much of an ideal after all. For these people get more out of life than the world's most cunning and wealthy sweater. King of gold-bags! A gipsy has forgotten more about the art of living than you will ever learn. A penniless, begging gipsy might well feel a sorrow and a pity for you.

Along over far-stretching roads. Ever they are moving. Going to the north, south, east or west. Moving along in the air and sunshine. Moving along in the wind and the rain. Caring for nothing but freedom to come and go. Too wise to live in dark, foul-aired towns. Too wise to hurry and to bustle. Going slowly along.

Before them passes the world. To them is revealed the strange secrets that change has to tell. They are at one with the elements. They fear them not.

These fine people of change. They are the wisest people in the whole of this mysterious world.

The slaves of no man. Freedom is for them more than life.

They care not for tomorrow, for tomorrow has not yet come. They care neither for fame nor gold nor titles nor opinions. They wish but to wander.

Go, gipsies. God be with you!

2

Concerning Friends.

OFTEN WHEN A MAN IS in a tight place he thinks how fine it would be to have a rich friend who would likely enough help him out of his difficulty. How good it would be to have a pal one could borrow the absolutely from whom necessary ten or twenty or hundred pounds! But the only people he knows are people of much the same financial status as himself. Even if they were ever so willing they could do nothing for him.

If there were only some wealthy man who really liked him! Why, the thing could be settled at once. Armed with the hundred pounds, that his friend would lend him, he would be able to stop his place from being sold up! And he goes along feeling moody and desperate. There is no one to whom he can turn. It is hard! Yes, it is very hard. But I have my doubts as to a rich friend being really able to help him, even if he had one who was willing to do so.

There are more poor men who have rich friends than one might suppose. For genuine friendship depends on other things than equality of financing status. A rich man is after all a human being. He has his likes and dislikes just as men have who haven't a sovereign to bless themselves. And it sometimes happens that circumstance throws him into contact with a poor man whom he gets to like. And the poor man likes him in return.

They are friends. I mean friends in the real and finest sense. But the friendship is a somewhat difficult matter for both. For when the poor man is in a tight place he would not be human did he not think now and then of the ease with which his rich friend could get him out of that tight place. And if the rich man has a heart—which sometimes happens—he must also think of it, that is, if the matter is brought to his notice.

But helping his friend is not as easy as it looks. Giving him the hundred, or whatever is needful, may have a tendency to undermine his self-reliance and his fighting power. In this world one has to fight all the time. And anything that is calculated to diminish a man's fighting power is dangerous.

There is a risk therefore of the rich man turning his friend into a follower and a hanger-on, if he gives or lends him money.

The whole situation is difficult.

I am talking now of rich men who are sympathetic and considerate towards those they like, who chance to be not well off. But there are rich men who have consideration for no one, not even for those they like. Of these friends a poor man ought to beware altogether. They are absolutely of no use to him at all. Indeed they are a harm.

I mean the rich friend who shows the trend of his character by the way he leaves you to settle a big cab fare. He is so used to vast sums that small trifles such as this escape his notice. A man who thinks in thousands can't take the same financial view as the man who thinks but in shillings.

And sometimes a rich friend is mean. Even though he rolls in wealth he has never been able to shed the meanness from his character the meanness that got him his first start. He reckons everything up, and often sees to it that you pay your share.

He likes you, and he wastes your time and your energy. He has you around and about and here and there with him when you ought to be attending to the forwarding of your own affairs.

In a word, this rich friend of yours sponges off you. And if you are wise, you will cut him. If you don't, he will ruin you.

Many a clever and talented man has been ruined by rich friends. They have got everything from him, and given him nothing in return. They have taken him so much away from his work that the time at last came when the power to do this work was gone. And he fell, and was lost.

Having rich friends is also apt to make you discontented. You go to their beautiful houses and over their wide parks and domains, and you can't help but feel how small and poor is your own establishment. You ought not to feel like this. But you do. You can't help it. You like this man. But the fact is that compared with him you have nothing. And discontented thoughts arise in you, however you may try to repress them.

And so you get wondering as to how you can make money in vast sums yourself. For you also would like to have a yacht and a beautiful house and grounds and horses. You would like to be able to go at any time you like to any part of the world. You feel cramped by your poverty, or your comparative poverty.

When a rich man, who is a good sort, is asked by his friend who is poor to lend him a sum of money he is placed in a very difficult position. If he does not lend it, the friendship is broken or at least it is injured. For, naturally, when a man is in a hole he has no use for a friend who won't help to pull him out of it. The reasons for the friend not doing so may be the best reasons in the world. But if you are in a hard plight, you have no patience to listen to the long and sound views that may be put forward by the person who can easily help you out of the plight, but won't. Human nature is human nature. And, if I may so put it, it lives largely from hand to mouth. I mean that people judge men and circumstances practically by the way they affect them in times of necessity. You say to yourself, "Here am I, at my wits' end, and this rich man, who is my friend, won't help me." And you are vexed, and you close your heart and your sympathies against him.

I know that it cuts but a little figure with you to remind you that this would not happen were your friend poor. But such is the fact. You make a demand upon him because he has money. And you are vexed with him when he does not comply with this demand. You have no more right to make this demand upon him than you would have if he were as poor as yourself. You are not treating him fairly.

And still you are. He ought to help you out of your difficulty, for what good is a friend if he leaves you in the lurch?

But listen:

This man had friends before, and whenever he helped them out of a money difficulty, it turned out invariably that he lost their friendship through it. Something came up—either there was an awkwardness because the money was not paid back, or there were further requests—and in the end the friendship was broken.

This is the reason he won't help you. It is a good reason.

But you care not the snap of a finger for it.

And so it is. The friendship of a rich man for a poor man is hedged around with the most tremendous difficulties, even though the rich man be one of the best fellows going. Indeed it seems to me to be almost impossible for it to exist.

And still circumstances often bring rich men and poor men on a plane of equality. And as real friendship depends only upon men instinctively liking each other, it may happen that they become friends.

But the friendship is all but impossible to keep.

It is an odd thing, but sometimes one's enemy turns out to be a good friend.

By this I do not mean that the enemy changes his spots. Not at all. I mean that some malicious act of your enemy stimulates you to make an effort, and your success dates from the time of that act.

Very likely you have been slack. Very likely you have been letting things go by the board. You are going downhill. Your friend is sympathetic and lends you money, the only result of which is to make things worse for you. For when the time comes you are unable to pay it hock. It only adds to the already heavy burden that oppresses you.

And along comes your enemy—the one who is instinctively and actively against you. He doesn't like you, and you don't like him. And he says something, or does something that is calculated to make things harder for you.

And lo! you suddenly put your back into the conduct of your affairs. You pull things out of the fire. You are stimulated in a curious way. And things take a turn. You are once more sailing before a fair wind.

I don't know if this has ever happened to you. But it has happened to me. I look back into my life and see where I have actually been done good by some inimical act, or some hard word, or some sneer. At the time I was put about and hurt. But when I think of it now, I could almost find it in me to shake hands with the person who had without intending it done me a good turn.

It is useless to deny it. There are people who are one's natural enemies. It is often impossible to love your neighbor as yourself. Your natural enemy may be a far finer and nobler and more honest and better character than you are. And still you don't like him. You detest the sight of him. His very virtues irritate you.

Of course, you ought to like him. But, sad to relate, life is not run on copybook maxims. You dislike him, and he dislikes you. And there is the end of it.

Noble-browed philosophers, who have dealt in lofty and beautiful thoughts, have often deplored this. But alas! I fear that these noble-browed philosophers were but people who knew what was good—for everyone but themselves. For from what I have heard they had their lives and dislikes. In this sense they were at one with the people with low foreheads.

The truth of the matter is that people may be likened to notes in music. Some notes are in accord, others are in disaccord. Some people are in accord. Some are not. You see a man, and you like him at once. And you think what a fine fellow he is. He is probably no such thing. He may be the biggest ruffian unhung. But he is one who, given the right circumstances, would be a friend of yours.

It is all a case of temperament. By temperament I mean the effect of the sum total of yourself. If two sum totals agree it is all right. If not, it is all wrong.

If you are at all sensitive you will know at the instant of meeting whether you like a person or not. If you don't like a person at the instant of meeting, it is wiser, if possible, not to have anything more to do with them. For as sure as you do, you will rue it.

There are people who are too dull and insensitive to know whether or not they like others when they first meet them. And these are the people who are always changing their friends. They are always being deceived in people! The fact is that it is they themselves who are to blame. They had no right ever to become intimate with the people with whom they have just fallen out.

It is said that some people are incapable of forming friendships with anyone. But I don't think that this happens often. However morose, or cross-grained you are there is always someone whom you will like, and who will like you. So don't despair. Of course there are people who have a strong capacity for friendship. There are some people who are more in tune with common humanity than others. They are people who possess the mysterious faculty that is called magnetism. It is easy for them to make friends. Never run away with the idea that a man is a bad sort, just because you don't like him. He may be a hundred times better than you are yourself. And if he turns out to be your enemy he is not necessarily a villain. It doesn't follow that he is everyone's enemy, just because he is yours. And don't go warning people against him. It is foolish. Remember that no one who has sense pays attention to you. Realize that he is simply a person who was born in disagreement with yourself. I don't mean to suggest that you must follow the copybook maxim and take him to your bosom. I mean that you must realize that this world is a big world, and that there are a good many people in it, and that the mystery of likes and dislikes is beyond the power of the human mind to solve.

An odd fact in the relationships between human beings is this. It is often possible for you to like two people who dislike each other. They appeal to you in altogether different ways. And one of the hard things to bear with in life is when one of these people expects you to be unfriendly with the other just because they are unfriendly with them. A man or a woman as much as says to you: "I want you to dislike this person because I dislike them."

This unfair and unreasonable attitude is most difficult to contend with. It causes a good deal of the bother and trouble in life.

I am not saying that people should not take sides. You must take sides in serious matters. You must at times become a partisan. But between taking sides in a serious difference, and disliking people just at the bidding of other people, there is a far cry.

Life is a very mixed-up game indeed. And all that the wisest philosopher has ever been able to do is to make bad guesses concerning the solution of its problems.

A friend may turn out to be the very worst enemy you have ever had. I don't mean intentionally. I mean his influence upon your life may be ruinous. He may do you helpful turns when it would have been far better for you had he left you to sink or swim yourself.

Everyone has to fight his own battle. It is the law of life that there is no getting behind. If your battle is not a battle for bread, it is some other battle. And you must fight it yourself. No friend can help you. What you really need is perhaps a spur.

And this is more apt to come from an enemy.

3

Putting On Side!

T HE MAN WHO HAS THE POWER within him to be successful in the struggle of life is invariably accused of putting on side. It is said of him that he is no longer the same to his old associates—that he looks down upon them. The men he knew in the old days—who still remain in their old places—say that when he sees them in the street now, he passes them by without noticing them, or that he, at most, bestows upon them a patronizing nod that galls them. And they speak to others of the old days when he used to be glad to know them, and indeed—so some of them assert—borrow money of them which they suggest has not all been paid back. They talk very bitterly of this man who refuses to be hail-fellow-well-met with his old friends. In a word, they accuse him of putting on side.

Putting on side! It is a slang phrase with a great deal of meaning in it. Its meaning is difficult to define exactly. It is used in a reproachful sense, suggesting that a man is ungrateful and forgetful and unfair and a user of others, and a snob.

It is a hard phrase to fling at a man who attains to the thing that is called success. And it is one of the things that the man of success feels, for there is no man so unsociable as not to wish to be thought well of by his fellows—at least he most certainly has this wish in the beginning of his success. Nearly all men, taking them all round, are good fellows who would like to do well by the people they know. The man who says otherwise is no judge of human nature. Study what is called a selfish man, and you will find that almost always his selfishness springs from a cause outside of himself. Men like to be thought well of by men.

I will admit now—not for the sake of argument, but I will admit it frankly—that successful men do, usually, put on side. The accusation made against them by those who have failed to make their point in life is perfectly true. A successful man puts on side.

But it is not his fault.

It is forced upon him by those who have failed. They have driven him into doing it. They have forced him to put on side in sheer self-defense. They have made him erect this barrier between himself and themselves because of their assaults upon him. There is a saying to the effect that it is easy failure—but difficult to sympathize with success. I don't know who it was that said this, but the sayer of it was one who had an acute knowledge of human nature. People who know you as a rule are sorry for you when you are down. They may consider you a bit of a nuisance when you go and ask them to back up their sorrow concerning you by the lending to you of money, but people are in the main good-hearted, and being so they don't like to see you hard up or cast down because of your failure in the game of life. They feel a pity for you even when they become tired and refuse to lend you any more money. This aptitude for pity is one of the beautiful things in human nature, and is really the cause of the world going round, so to speak. It is why hospitals are built, and why people go and do self-sacrificing and generous things. But for this trait in humanity, the halt and the maim and the blind would never get a chance at all in this hard world. Be hard up and in trouble, and some one or another will surely help—that is, if you let them know your condition. Ask and you shall receive, said Christ.

But make your own way, win in the game, and you will find that your old friends usually show you the hard, critical face. You will want to keep well with them, but you will find it all but impossible. They find fault with you for the least thing. Things that you did when you were hard up and unsuccessful without attracting the slightest attention now call for sharp criticism in these, your days of success. You will find amongst other things that your income is put at least three times as much as it actually is. An old friend drops in on you to borrow money, and won't believe you when you tell him what is the truth that you haven't got it. By accident you fail to see a man on the street, and he accuses you of doing it designedly. You greet a man and he feels that your greeting isn't strong enough. You make a joke, and it is construed into a sneer. Your time is limited now because there is so much call upon it and that, too, gives offence. You ought to loaf away the hours as you did in your old, unsuccessful days! You give offence because you have stopped drinking whisky, and therefore refuse to go into dram-shops with those with whom you wasted time in the old days. Perfect strangers, or nearly perfect strangers, are vexed because you don't respond enthusiastically when they slap you on the back.

In a word, you are subjected to criticism of a most unfair kind.

You may be the kind of successful man who realizes that success is necessarily gained at the expense of others—that other people's faults and weaknesses are your gain—that if everyone were as sharp and as strong as you are you wouldn't be successful. But the realizing of this won't help you in the least. You may feel very sorry indeed for those you have beaten in the race, but your sorrow won't be appreciated. You will find that the fellows who were so nice and friendly to you in the old days have changed in their manner. I am not saying that there won't be a very few who are friendly towards you, but these are very, very few indeed.

Of course, the reason of this attitude is easy enough to understand. There are not enough prizes to go round in the world. Everybody can't win the race. And the reason of your old friends' attitude towards you is because they feel jealous and envious at not having won the prize that you have won. They would never admit this were you to tax them with it, but the fact, nevertheless, remains. They are consciously, or unconsciously, jealous and envious of you. And they justify their unfair attitude towards you by accusing you of things of which you are no more guilty than the babe unborn. Whatever you do, you can't please them. Be as civil and as considerate as you may, and they are not satisfied.

Success has made you a kind of an Ishmael at least, amongst the majority of your old friends.

You feel this deeply, for you are probably one who feels that old friends are the best friends. You would like to keep on with them, and it hurts you very much indeed when they accuse you falsely of ignoring, or patronizing them—of putting on side. But it is of no use. You can do nothing.

And in the end you become hardened. You must protect yourself. And you become really guilty of the crime of which you have been so long accused.

You put on side.

4

Men Who Are Down.

I T IS A HARD THING for a man to be down. It is a hard
thing for a man to be broken and lost and to feel that the chances
are against his being able to regain his feet.

People there are who say that it is a man's own fault. But these
people are either ignorant or without heart.

It may be that you were one who helped to build up into success
some gigantic enterprise. It may be that you gave to it the best of your
life and your effort, and that you were flung aside when the power
was sapped out of you. In these days of vast industrial enterprises
such tragedies happen every day. Men are used and cast aside as are
cast aside broken tools.

So it is well for people to think twice before they say it is a man's
own fault for being down.

Or you may have committed a crime. And you are down because
of that. No one will look at you. No one will give you work. There is
no one to help you. And so you are a man who is broken and lost.

But let me tell the people who would cast stones at such a man
that the worst crimes against our social order are never punished.

The worst criminals live in the midst of ease and splendor and honor. The ruler of one of the greatest of the world's states has lately given it forth in public that the predatory rich are more dangerous to society even than Anarchists. So also think twice before you cast stones at the man who is called a criminal. And remember that the possibilities of crime are in all of us. The man who denies that they are in him is either a hypocrite or a fool.

If you are not sorry for the man who has been broken because of a crime he has committed, at least be fair. For he is most likely as good a man as you are. The main thing is that he has been more unfortunate. Do something for him if you can. If you cannot do anything, be good enough not to sneer. I repeat, he is as good a man as you are.

It is sometimes thought that men who are down are men who are essentially weak. But this is not always so. Circumstance is stronger than the strongest man. You may be a man of power and force and you may be down. You may be a brilliant man and you may be down. Or a man of marked ability. The reason for your being down may have been because of a certain nobility in your character. You were not a liar. You were not one who would cringe. And because of this you were pushed aside.

I have personally known strong and able and clever men who have had to beg their bread. I have known men who were willing to work and who could get no work. This talk of there being work for every man who is willing to work is untrue, and what is more the people who indulge in it know that it is untrue. The truth of the matter is that the army of unemployed is growing day by day, because machinery is being used to do the work that was once done by men. And this is the chief reason why I have so often said that machinery is a curse. Machinery would not be the curse to mankind that it is at present were it not for the fact that the benefit arising from its use is stolen by a few cunning men. Machinery is being used to starve and oppress and crush mankind. This truth cannot be put forth too often.

WHEN YOU ARE BROKEN AND down the world is for you an awful world of darkness. You are here in the light amongst your fellows, and still you are as if chained down in some dark pit.

You wander along the streets, hungry. Life for you is one long pain and misery. If you had the courage you would end it all. But you have not the courage. You are dispirited and weak and broken.

It may well be that if you have come from the prison you will wish yourself back again. There at least you had food and shelter of a kind. You are free now, but your freedom is a mockery.

It may be that you had a family in the old days when you were on your feet. As you go sadly along you wonder what has become of them. What has become of your son? What happened to your daughter? What happened to them years ago when disgrace and shame fell upon you? When you passed through the prison gate they were not there to see you. You could bear them not being there did you feel that they were getting on all right. You could bear them being too much ashamed to come and see you when you left the prison. But the thought that they, too, may be lost and broken is too much for you to bear.

There are good, strong, capable men who have never had a chance. You may have talent and ability and energy, but if you are born in the wrong set these faculties may well become your undoing. A smart, clever lad of the slums may be in danger of becoming a criminal. This same lad if sent to a public school and to the university would turn out in an altogether different way. If his parents were well off his faculties would be given every chance to develop. A seat would be got for him in Parliament and he would be pushed and helped in every way possible. He would be noticed in Parliament because of his talent, and he would get on.

And so it goes. One lad is put right on the way to destruction, the other lad gets every imaginable chance. The proverb that says every man has a chance is the biggest lie that has ever masqueraded as a wise saying. You might as well say that a child who is brought up half-starved in a tenement has as good a chance of growing up to be a healthy man as a child who lives in a fine house in the country and who gets all he wants to eat. So when you see the men who are broken and down, think a little before you blame them. Do not forget that the same fate might have been your own—in fact, that it may be your own. Circumstance is a very big word indeed. It laid even Napoleon by the heels.

Be sorry for the men who are down. And if you are so case-hardened[13] that you are not sorry for them, at least try to be fair.

---

13 "Case-hardening" is the process of hardening the surface of a metal object while allowing the metal deeper underneath to remain soft, thus forming a thin layer of harder metal (called the "case") at the surface. However, because hardened metal is usually more brittle than softer metal, it is not always a suitable choice. Often used as a metaphor for a person without compassion.

5

Police And Criminals.

THE POLICE ARE FAR MORE fair and just in their
personal attitude towards the class known by the generic name
of criminals than are the general public.

And here let it not be thought that I am an apologist for the
police. I am not. I am utterly against them. They are the rulers of
this beautiful civilization. But one must be fair even to those whom
one does not exactly care about.

And it is only fair to repeat that in practice the police act with
more decent feeling, with more pity, with more sense of justice, with
more recognition of common humanity towards the unfortunates
who are called criminals than do the general public.

Mind you, I do not deny that when the police have a man they
will try to keep him. And often, scoundrelly things will be done to
keep him. But the police do not act in this way just because they are
police. They act in this way because they are human beings. And the
merest tyro in the study of human beings knows that the strongest
instinct in a clique or a class is to stick together. To stick together
a clique or a class will stretch all sorts of points. Lies will be told,

questionable acts will be excused. As we know, this happens all the time in politics, and in governing affairs. Let me put it like this: Suppose a man deeply wrongs another man, and suppose the punishing of this man endangers or discredits the clique or the body to which he belongs! Well, what happens? Why, there is an effort made to gloss the affair over. The clique invariably considers its own interests before it considers the interests of justice. This has happened and always will happen as long as cliques—especially ruling cliques—are formed amongst human beings.

I am quite sure that perjury is often committed by the police. But I say, also, that if you and I, and others of the general public, were made into policemen, there would be times when we, ourselves, would commit perjury. We would not be able to get out of it. We would find, when we were included in the governing ring, that there would come at some time or another a moment when circumstances would bend us.

The time will, of course, come when men will refuse to be pushed and bossed about by policemen. But at present they exist, and it is only fair to state that they are in themselves no worse than other people. Indeed, in one great respect they are a great deal better. They are personally fairer and more just and humane towards the unfortunate people who are called criminals.

T HE PEOPLE WHO ARE CALLED criminals are at present treated by Society in a most cruel and atrocious manner. A man commits an act of crime and often the wrong that Society inflicts upon him is a thousand times greater than the wrong he has committed. And even after he has been punished atrociously for his crime, Society is guilty of the deepest and most cruel injustice of all towards him. Society treats him as a leper. He is cast out. He is marooned.

It is all very well to rail at the cruelty that goes on in prisons, and to hold one's hands up in horror when one hears of what goes on in places like the Devil's Island[14]. But these places are but expressions of the attitude of Society in general towards the unfortunates who are called criminals.

Take a case in point: A well-placed man in English Society commits a crime that is found out. It may not be really a crime at all in the truly criminal sense. The bother he is in may have been brought about by circumstances over which he had no control. He goes to prison. He is punished and broken. His family is scattered.

After he has come out of prison, does Society help him? No! He is treated with the grossest and most cold-blooded unfairness. And there is no good reason for treating him as he is treated. Sometimes men have the hypocrisy and the effrontery to say that he must be cast out so that Society may be protected. But these men in their hearts know that bigger and worse criminals than this unfortunate man ever knew how to be are crowned with honors by this very Society.

The fair thing, of course, would be to take this man after he came out of prison and, as nearly as possible, reinstate him in his old position. If he belonged to a good club he should be taken back again. It would be an act of bare and simple fairness. But what club in London would do it?

---

14 Devil's Island (*Île du Diable*) was the nickname of a French penal colony named Bagne de Cayenne that operated in the 19th and 20th centuries in the Salvation's Islands of French Guiana. It was infamous for its harsh treatment of detainees, with a death rate of 75% at their worst, until it was closed in 1953. Devil's Island was notorious for being used for the internal exile of French political prisoners, with the most famous being Captain Alfred Dreyfus. Henri Charrière's bestselling book *Papillon* (1969) describes his successful escape from Devil's Island with a companion, Sylvain. It was made into a successful film of the same name in 1973 starring Steve McQueen as Charrière, Dustin Hoffman as Sylvain, and Woodrow Parfrey as Clusiot.

No, the prison horrors that we hear about are but the results of the cruel and cowardly attitude of Society towards the unfortunate.

It is not the jailers who torture prisoners. It is Society.

THIS IS THE POINT I am coming to: The police never act in so dreadful a manner as this towards those who have been in prison. They never look upon these people as lepers. They may be unfair to them; they may sometimes take advantage of them.

But they always recognize that they are human beings.

Men who have been unfortunate know this. They know that the man who has hunted them down has no feeling of loathing towards them. Often the police help the unfortunates after they have come out of prison. And the help does not come in the insulting "holier than thou" manner. It comes as man to man.

The hardest thing of all that a man, who has done time, has to bear is the being treated as though he were a leper.

And whatever else the police are guilty of, they are not guilty of this. I am against the police. I would abolish them if I could.

But I respect and honor them for realizing that the unfortunates, who are called criminals, are human beings.

AND I WILL TELL YOU why the police do it. Their profession faces them with the fact that human beings are much alike, whether they are called criminal or not. They know, better than anyone else, that ninety-nine out of the hundred parts of crime are to be discovered in the words, "being found out."

A policeman may by nature be dull, but this fact is soon forced upon him. And so he loses the feeling of loathing for men who have been in prison. And he probably enough looks upon all people as possible criminals. Which is a most correct way to look at the whole matter.

And the more experience he has the more does he see that many a decent man has been in jail. He knows that many a man would run straight if Society only gave him the chance.

True, he hunts the criminal down. True, he is not always scrupulous in his methods. He is out to convict those who come into his hands.

But it is his business. It is the way he earns his bread. He looks at the game purely from the professional point of view.

If I may so put it, he is in such a position that he sees both sides of the social coin. And he sees that the only difference between the two sides is the difference of marking.

The metal is the same.

Perhaps he becomes a cynic. And what of it? It is good to be cynical. It means that the scales have fallen from your eyes.

The policeman knows that the genuine criminal is very rare indeed. And he knows also that he is born in no particular class. The genuine criminal may be a person with thousands a year. He knows also that the class that is called the criminal class is practically made up of people who get no real chance in life. He knows again that the proportion of real criminals, in this so-called criminal class, is smaller than it is in the wealthy, leisured class. How does the policeman get his knowledge?

Well, certainly not from treatises upon what is called criminal psychology. He has no use for such trash.

He gets his knowledge straight from life.

And so it is that he has no loathing for unfortunate men just because they have been in prison.

For experience has shown him that, taken altogether, they are just as good as other men.

6

Cynicisms.

M AN IS CONTINUALLY BOTHERED by problems. There is the great and pressing problem of how to get a first-class living by the doing of toil that is at once very light and very interesting. A problem that I, myself, have been trying to solve for years.

And there are other problems.

There is the problem of peace, and the problem of war. There is the problem of how to enjoy yourself in every possible way, and at the same time to keep fit and healthy. A more difficult problem to solve than usual. And if you are a nimble-witted extractor of the wealth of others, you are confronted with the problem of how to at once extract the wealth and at the same time to keep out of jail. This problem is easy enough to solve if you are a person of large ideas.

There is the problem that faces the idealist. You all know the idealist. He is the person who thinks that the world should be run on grand and beautiful and idyllic lines. He is satisfied with nothing. Or rather, he is satisfied with nothing but himself. The problem that faces him is the living up to his ideals. But alas! He makes but a poor hand at the solving of it. I have known a great many idealists. I have known a great many dealers in the word that is beautiful and noble and grand. And frankly, I must say that they, as a class, are the weirdest crowd of men that I have ever met in my somewhat varied career. Why an idealist is not potted at sight, it puzzles me to fathom. Compared with an idealist a bunco[15]-steerer is a deeply respectable person. Oh, why did not the renowned Dr. Johnson give a definition of the idealist in his immortal dictionary? He put the patriot in his right place, but the idealist could give even the patriot tips in ways that are deep and dark. Whenever I think of the idealist, I get vexed. For the idealist is simply an impudent person who thinks that he may commit all kinds of questionable acts just because he deals in beautiful and noble words. And the worst of it is that he never admits even to himself that he does anything wrong. He feels evidently that his noble sentiments give him a license to do what he likes. And I ask you, my reader—if you have ever had the misfortune to meet an idealist—to bear me out in this. But I must pass on. For if I say much more about the idealist I will forget myself and perhaps swear.

There is the problem of the suffrage for women. But about this problem I will say nothing, for I have dealt with it before. I will content myself only by repeating my humble plea to the women not to raise any more disturbances at Westminster. Dear women! Please remember that you are ladies! Don't raise disturbances, and the suffrage will come—in the sweet bye and bye.

There is the problem of how to make it appear to a deeply interested world that you are a great deal better off than you really are. I may say that this problem is peculiarly an English one. The desire to show

15 "Bunco" was originally a confidence game similar to three card monte. It originated in 19th-century England where it was known as "eight dice cloth." It was imported to San Francisco as a gambling activity in 1855, where it gave its name to gambling parlors, or "Bunco parlors," and more generally to any swindle. After the American Civil War the game evolved to a popular parlor game. During the 1920s and Prohibition, Bunco was re-popularized as a gambling game, often associated with a speakeasy. Law-enforcement groups raiding these parlors came to be known as "Bunco squads." Bunco as a family game saw a resurgence in popularity in the 1980s.

off, and appear very tony indeed, seems to be deeply ingrained in our national character. People of other nationalities take the views of their neighbors with more philosophy.

I have often wondered what will happen when all the problems are solved. How will politicians and thinkers and idealists get a living? Of course, I know that there are optimistic people who say that there will always be problems with us. But this surely can't be so. A time must come when man will be so wise that nothing will puzzle him. And what will happen then? Alas! I fear that the person with the large dome of thought, and the idealist, and the patriot will have to work for a living. But that dreadful time of universal wisdom is, at present, some distance off. And I am pleased. For how would I, myself, get a living if there were no burning questions for me to write upon? What would happen to me were there no ruffians who took a delight in coming down hard upon humanity? Why, upon me would fall disaster. I would have to lay down the pen and take up the pick and shovel.

It will be a sorry day for the thinker and the idealist and the patriot, and the rest of the people who really know what is what, when the problem vanishes. A very sorry day indeed. But, I am pleased to say, a very distant day.

All problems have one feature in common. Their solution is the easiest thing in the world. You, or the other person, have but to act in a certain way, and lo! the thing is solved. And this way is always clearly laid down by some disinterested person. This clear, sharp-sighted, disinterested person knows to a dot just how things should be done.

I am sometimes puzzled at the existence at all of problems in a world so full of clear and disinterested advice. Still, as I pointed out, it is not for me to grumble. Neither is it for the idealist nor the person with the bulging dome of thought to grumble.

I wonder if animals have problems. But the thought at once comes to me that animals do not possess intellect. They only possess sense.

As near as I can get at it, man has always had problems to solve. But he was not always so easy in his attitude towards the disinterested problem-solver as he is at present. In the old, ancient, moss-covered days he had a distaste for expert advice regarding the problems that confronted him. If you told a landlord that he ought to give up his land, and go and do a bit of work for a living, he quite often looked upon your advice as being in the nature of a rudeness. As the Americans say, the expert adviser had often to light out quick. It wasn't so easy in those good old ancient days to slap a king or an emperor on the back—if I may use so daring a metaphor—and tell him a thing or two about running his show. The common people were also a bit uncertain in their attitude towards the one who knew exactly on what lines the world should be run.

The old ancient mossy days were sorry days for the problem-solvers. But now happily all this is over. The world brims with exact advice about everything. If you are an emperor, and things don't go like clockwork, all you have to do is to peruse the writings of some noble and thoughtful person, and you will receive tips of the most invaluable character. If you are a landlord, and you are bothered by some intelligent person who won't pay rent, the same sort of thing will happen. If you are a millionaire, and the problem of your wealth annoys you, why, all you have to do is to communicate with some such problem-solver as myself—and you will be told what to do with at least some of your money.

Yes, the world teems with exact and definite advice about every mortal thing. And the solution of the most difficult problem is as easy as falling off a log.

All you have to do is to take the advice that is so freely and generously offered.

It must be plain even to the most feeble intellect that laws in the beginning were simply the mandates that the conquerors laid down for the conquered.

After the conquerors had killed enough people, they came to the conclusion that killing might as well stop, so they issued a mandate, or law, to the effect that from then on everyone should live with his neighbor in amity and peace and beautiful harmony. The conquerors were human enough not to relish the idea of the conquered turning the tables upon them. No one likes a dose of one's own medicine. And the conquerors began to see that killing was even more than an impoliteness.

They began to see that it was rude.

True, they themselves had done all sorts of things. There were times even when they had gone at dead hours of the night and killed people. And a person of a nice, legal turn of mind might have reminded them of this when they were framing their excellent law. But in those simple days the lawyer did not occupy the center of the floor. He had not yet come into his own.

It was the same way about stealing.

After the conquerors had stolen everything they could see, they came to the conclusion that from then on stealing was a base and ignoble piece of business. A mean piece of business. It pained and saddened them to think that the persons from whom they had stolen everything should even as much as dream of stealing a bit of their own back. So out came another law.

It is all very well for sour critics to make rude remarks about human nature. It is all very well for crabby and dyspeptic thinkers to grumble.

But virtue must have a beginning.

And that the conception of the virtue of honesty arose in the minds of men, after they had stolen everything in sight, is in itself nothing against the inherent beauty that lies in honesty. Out of evil comes good. From the dark soil comes the beautiful flower.

The bold and skillful thieves, who invented the virtue of honesty, also let loose upon the world the following beautiful aphorism of pearly wisdom which still glistens and shines for the benefit of man: Honesty is the best policy!

And so the laws went on, till at last there was built up our present, many-gabled, legal structure.

As the laws were in the process of being built, complications set in. Some of the conquerors did rude things to their fellow-conquerors. And so by degrees there crept into the law-idea a thing called fairness. Truth to tell, however, this fairness was but as a beautiful woman who reserved her smiles for lawbreakers of the dominant, conquering class. If you were a lawbreaker of the conquered class she usually forgot to smile upon you. She turned her head the other way.

And it may also be said that fairness was not an inherent element of the law. It came but as an afterthought. And even then it was only introduced now and then.

In these righteous, modern days fairness still enters into the administration of the law.

If you have money!

Let it not be thought that I am one who has the hard word for lawyers. Let it not be thought that I am one who calls them rude names. In fact, when people say they are not honest, I always speak up in their defense.

For lawyers are honest. Indeed it would be hard for them to be otherwise.

For they possess the earth in its roundness.

And rightly. For they are the lineal descendants of the bold and skillful gentlemen who in the beginning invented the very virtue of honesty. I mean the gentlemen who let loose upon the world the glistening aphoristic pearl which goes to the effect that honesty is the best policy.

Again, the lawyer is a person who possesses what might be called the all-round, impartial mind. He is dowered with that truest kind of wisdom—the wisdom that realizes that all coins have two sides, and that one side of the coin is much the same as the other.

I admire him.

I am not one who thinks that it would be a good idea to raze to the ground the many-gabled, legal structure that stands in our midst. In a word, I would not, even if I could, do away with the laws that keep us so polite and honest and respectable. There was a time, I regret to say, when I thought all law was an abomination. But these Anarchistic views have left me. I am getting mellower and more sympathetic the more I see of life.

The laws give the robbers and thieves fixity of tenure. And no one with any sense will deny the fact that this is a good thing. It would be a great bother were we to be inflicted with the perpetual rowing that would ensue were robber always robbing robber. It would be impossible to sleep at nights.

Turnabout is fair play!

Ah! another aphorism. But I am beginning to be chary of aphorisms and proverbs. Deep study of aphorisms and proverbs has led me to the conclusion that they are but clever phrases invented by clever people for the purpose of imposing their wishes upon an innocent and gullible world. "Honesty is the best policy!" This beautiful phrase was invented by the bold and skillful gentlemen of ancient times after they had stolen all that was stealable. They also invented the phrase, "Thou shalt not kill!" after they had killed everyone in sight.

I am chary of proverbs and aphorisms, and I fear that "Turnabout is fair play!" was invented by the relations of the people who were killed, and by the people from whom everything had been stolen.

Let us salute the ancient and honorable thieves and killers of men who had the wit to invent laws!

Let us salute the inventors of virtue!

It may well be, of course, that the laws will be unable to ensure the robbers and thieves fixity of tenure for ever. But this is not the fault of the laws. It must be remembered that to keep humanity in the straight and law-abiding path for eternity is the tallest of tall orders.

But you may be certain that the dispensers of the laws will do their very best to accomplish it. You may be certain that the lawyers and police and judges, and the rest of the legal gentry, will fight hard against the natural processes of decay.

And who is the one who is hard-hearted enough to blame them? Surely not you or I. For they give us a quiet and happy and peaceful life. They know that if they did not rob us, some other ruffians would come and do it.

And when I come to ponder over the matter of the invention of the laws more deeply, I am lost in admiring wonder at the knowledge of human nature that was displayed by these ancient conquerors. They built not for a day! Rather did they build for a thousand years.

For their wondrous invention still preserves the elasticity and the freshness of its youth.

The people who have all, still have all. The beautiful jade, Fairness—whom they introduced as an afterthought—still reserves her smiles for lawbreakers of the dominant class.

And everything goes merrily and well. Society is a little old, I will admit, but it is still in a state of beautiful preservation.

All through the laws which in the beginning were the mandates that the conquerors laid down to the conquered.

I HAVE OFTEN WONDERED WHERE the tradesman got his ethics. For his ideas of honesty would make even old Fagin blush. He has forgotten more about the fine art of stealing than Dickens' trainer of pickpockets ever knew. And the world is fond of him, for the world does not hang him as it did Fagin. The world makes him a knight or a baronet—if he steals enough.

It is not for me to quarrel with the world in this matter. For the world has some deep reason for paying the tradesman the honor it pays him. But I have often wondered why it is that the world discriminates so much between Fagin and the grocer—we will call him the grocer for convenience! The grocer sands your sugar, poisons you, and subjects you to all sorts of things—and lo! he blossoms forth as a knight or a baronet!

I wonder why it is?

On the other hand Fagin steals—or trains someone to steal—some unconsidered trifle from you. He relieves you of your watch, or something like that. And, behold, he is locked up and severely punished. No knighthood or baronetcy for Fagin! In fact, he is very lucky indeed if he does not end his vivid career in quod.

Still, what would life be if there were not these deep riddles to solve? If everything were plain sailing, how bored one would get. Besides, what would the philosophers do if life were a straight thing easy of solution? How would they get either a living or fame? If life were easy, we would have no novelist like Balzac or philosopher like Carlyle. Where would even a brilliant thinker like myself be if 2 and 2 really made 4 and 4 and 4 really made 8? Nowhere! If honesty were really honesty, and theft were really theft, there would be absolutely no employment for the worthy people who know exactly what is what, and who tell the same to a more or less interested world.

Perhaps the main difference between a grocer and a thief who gets locked up, is that the grocer feels that he is really honest whilst the thief who gets locked up feels that he is a thief.

Again it may be said that grocery is an industry that is run on respectable, regular lines, whilst pickpocketry and burglary and the like is worked in an irregular and spasmodic fashion. The grocer is an artist in theft—an industrious, painstaking artist. He relieves you of your money without your knowing it. He is civility and politeness itself, whilst the burglar and the footpad have methods that are rude and crude.

The bungler gets locked up whilst the artist goes free. And rightly.

I have just said that the grocer is civil and polite. But this I must modify. He is only civil and polite when he is actually robbing you. Should you turn the tables upon him he becomes as a roaring lion. No footpad or burglar is half so awful a person as the grocer who can't get his bill. He knows better even than a jailer how to make you feel that life is after all but a sorry and drab affair. Under his attentions you begin to see that suicide is a soothing and blessed idea. And I am sure that if criminals were sentenced to periods of dunning instead of being sent to jail honest crime would quickly disappear.

And should you ever owe a grocer a bill, and you haven't the money to pay him, take my advice and go forth and steal it. For I have been there. I mean I have owed a grocer money. And I am free to confess that if I could have cracked a crib or a safe, I would gladly have done so. For the man seemed to need his money with such urgency that I became interested. I never knew anybody who needed money as badly as that man. I dream of him even now. Oh, how he needed his money!

What a pity it is that the great genius, Shakespeare, did not make Shylock a grocer dunning for his bill instead of a moneylender demanding a mere pound of flesh! Surely he must have known grocers. Why did he not make his interesting hero a grocer? Why?

How cooing and gentle and kind and nice is the grocer when first you know him. How big he makes you feel. Under the spell of his seductive manner it comes to you that you are at the very least a cross between a demi-god and a king. Oh, he is so kind! And when he sends you in his first request to settle his bill. How civil and courteous and engaging is his request. The style of a Chinese editor, when he refuses a poem from a would-be contributor, is but a rude and abrupt style when compared with the style of the grocer's first request to settle his little bill. If the statesmen of the world were to get grocers to draft their diplomatic documents I am sure that wars would vanish.

In fact, so beautiful and poetic is his request that you feel that it would be a vulgarity to comply with it. It is impossible to think of pounds, shillings and pence in connection with this delicate and poetic missive. It would be profanation. It makes you feel that you are conferring the highest honor you possibly can upon this grocer by owing him money. Paying him? Why, it would be a rudeness. Besides, if you don't pay him you may have the luck to get in the fulness of time a similar missive.

But you never do.

For the second missive—well, there is a difference. But it is beyond my power to describe it properly. All that I can say is that it has nothing in it of the charm and delicacy of the missive that came to you first. It is not that it is rude. But there is a vague something in it that makes you feel that you might as well brass up. But you find that you can't brass up—for money is tight with you just at present. So you dismiss the subject from your mind. Or rather, you try to dismiss it. For the fact that you owe the grocer a bill keeps coming up when you are thinking of such subjects as how to become famous, or how to get rich quick. There was something in that second missive that fixed the fact indelibly in your mind that you owe him money. Not that it was rude. Oh, no. But something.

The third missive! Ah, it is a scorcher. And how the hand penned it that penned the first missive is to you a mystery. You can't imagine how the same mind could have conceived it. But there it is in black and white. You look at it, and look at it again. And upon you comes a fear. You throw it in the fire. But that does no good. You can still see it before you.

And the fourth! And the fifth! And then they come. And you begin to feel an interest in life such as you never thought you were capable of.

And at last you come to the point where, if you are wise, you will go forth and burgle for the money to meet this bill. This bill! Heavens! It is awful!

But why pursue a painful subject?

We all, alas! have been there!

When I go to another, and, I trust, a better world, I hope I will be able to pay for everything on the nail.

I started out by wondering where the tradesman, or, rather, the grocer, got his ethics. But I fear I must still wonder. For in writing I found that no ideas of an ethical character came to my mind as I concentrated it upon the grocer.

THE SHOUTING, UNATHLETIC CROWD that watches strong men, playing a rough and dangerous game of skill—or that watches two trained men fighting—bears no relation to these men. That is, the shouting crowd bears no relation to these men in the sense of being quick and strong and brave themselves. Indeed, the quicker and the braver and the stronger the professionals are, the worse is it for the crowd.

In this sense: The units of the crowd are apt to be discouraged by the skill and the hardihood of the professional combatants. I mean discouraged in the attempt to follow their example. They feel that it is impossible to do what these men do. And so they are content just to watch them, and to talk about them.

The physique and skill and courage of the professional is far removed from the physique and courage and skill of the average man. The professionals are in no way typical of the slack and puny people who watch them.

Such is the state of the masses in the physical sense. And whilst it is not to be claimed that it is quite symbolical of the state of the masses in the mental sense, thinking of it may well bring this fact to the mind: That the masses are kept, intellectually, at a standstill by a few people of powerful intellect, or by the processes that these people have invented in the past.

All the boasted inventions of civilization, such as reading and writing and mathematics, and votes, and machines, and electric bells, and the financial system, and tramcars and motor cars, are less than nothing—that is, in the sense of being a reflection of the mental power of the masses. And it must be clear, to even the feeblest thinker, that the present-day masses of England can't be nearly so intelligent as were the masses, say of a thousand years ago.

When I say masses, I also include those who have suffered the disadvantage of having received an expensive education. In fact, this select portion of the masses is composed of bigger fools than usual. And if they had to earn their living without favor, they would be nowhere. Public schools and colleges are essentially brain-chloroforming institutions. Of course, we get our rulers from them. Of course.

I wish to point out, however, that I do not hanker after the idyllic life of a thousand years ago. To say such a thing would be rude. Always be polite in speaking of the age in which you have the honor to live. Besides, by all accounts, life in the idyllic age of a thousand years ago was a bit rough. In that age there was no such person as the dear old British bobby to guide the steps of the feeble. The feeble person of a thousand years ago was now and then subjected to rudeness. And even the strong person had to keep a bright look-out. No, I think the present age, where intelligence is scientifically chloroformed, is by far the easiest age for a man like myself who has had the extreme good fortune to be uneducated.

It may be pointed out that in fighting a civilized people are superior to a savage people. And the civilized nonentity will perhaps be foolish enough to point with pride to the fact that the white men have beaten the Indians, or the Arabs.

But all that this really shows is that the white men have been able to take advantage of these people by murder-machines. And even the foolish, civilized nonentity is not fool enough to assert that in fair, hand-to-hand combat a machine-ridden white man would be a match for an Arab or an American Indian. The assertive and un-modest American knows that, man for man, the Indians were better fighters than white men. In fact, they were better men in every way than the average white man. The present-day Americans are indeed a parlous lot when compared with the fine people they murdered by the aid of machinery.

However, this is not quite the thing I wish to say. I merely wish to point out that the inventions of civilization lower the physique and the intelligence of the masses. And also I wish to make clear the fact that the advance of civilization is not an advance at all. It is a retrogression—a going back. Our whole system of education is, for example, too foolish for words.

The schoolmaster is a deadly blight that should be suppressed. And if it should ever come to pass that he should rule England, then, all I can say is goodbye, England. I am not much gone on the ruling business, but I must in justice say that the stupid people of the alleged upper classes are fitter to rule England than schoolmasters. I prefer the stupidity of the foxhunting squire to the brilliance of the schoolmaster every time. The English gentleman is dull beyond power of description, but there are times when he possesses the saving grace of being dimly aware that he is dull. And, anyway, he is never so dull as not to know that the only way to keep England is by fighting. And I may say further that some of the alleged upper-class people have the advantage of being practically illiterate. They have managed to keep their small speck of intelligence from being snuffed out by the process of education.

A humorous thing to me is the way that the people of civilization wish to confer the blessings of the civilized state upon uncivilized and savage peoples. But even the densest Digger Indian[16] knows that the white man has less than nothing to tell him.

Missionaries are also comedians of a rare and gifted order. And whenever I hear of them being eaten I am consoled by the fact that savages appreciate humor in so practical and wholehearted a way. And it occurs to me that it is the greatest pity that the simple and appreciative savage can't get a chance to interview the subtler humorist who provides the money to send the missionary comedians forth.

And here let me say a word to the guileless and simple reformer who thinks that the lot of mankind will be alleviated by education. I know you are honest, my good friend. But I also know that you are innocent. And your honesty and innocence make me afraid.

Listen! The world is too full of education already. The schoolmaster should be put to carrying the hod. The world is too full of readymade formulas that masquerade under the name of ideas. The world is too full of phrases and proverbs and aphorisms that either mean nothing, or that were designed for the especial purpose of hoodwinking the masses. I know that if you could only get into Parliament you would work wonders. But cleverer men than you have failed when they tried to make 5 out of 2 and 2.

The fact of the matter is that, mentally, the masses of civilization are kept where they are for the advantage of what might be called professional men of intellect and their descendants and followers. And the aim of all education is, broadly speaking, to keep them there. I have in my mind now a country where education is what

---

16   "Digger Indian" is an offensive disparaging term used predominantly during the 19th century referring to indigenous people of the Great Basin in the western United States (e.g., Utes, Paiutes, and Shoshone).

you might call rampant. And the people of that country are really more enslaved than the people of any other country.

The savage and uncivilized races, as we impolitely term them, get far more out of life than do we—the proud possessors of a beautiful and luminous civilization. That is, they get more out of life if they have the good luck to be able to keep us off from them.

No social system or state can be really worth anything where the paramount aim is not to allow the individual to develop to the fullest, both mentally and physically. And this aim has never been the aim of any civilized state. As I said, this reading and writing, and electric bells and telegraphy, and all kinds of enginery, and, if you like, flying ships, mean less than nothing when they are acquired at the expense of the development of the individual.

The aim of all civilized states has been to keep the masses in subjection for the benefit of cliques. And this is as true of republics as it is of autocracies. In fact the ruling clique of a republic is more unconscionable than the ruling clique of an autocracy. The money clique that rules America is more oppressive and horrible than is the Grand Ducal clique of Russia. It has a far worse effect upon the American character. The reason of this is that the Grand Dukes are by long odds better men than the American money kings. They have more sense of responsibility towards the community upon which they batten.

Man is more of a man in the social state that is called savage and uncivilized.

Civilization is but a vast, theatric, backward step in the social life of humanity.

THE MORALITY THAT HAS BEEN invented to guide the individual is at once exact and narrow and comprehensive. It is impossible for you to go wrong, if you will only keep your weather eye on it.

You are not to tell lies, you are not to kill, you are not to steal, you are not to think ill of people or feel revengeful against people, in fact, you are not to do numberless things. If you go wrong, you go wrong with your eyes wide open. And the punishment that falls upon you for going wrong is well deserved. For you can't say that you were not warned.

When I think of the way that the individual is fathered and mothered by the school and the Church and the State and the poet and the idealist and the professional moralist and the profound thinker and the subtle writer, I am astonished that he should ever stray from the paths of rectitude. When I go to the courts and gaze upon the lofty-browed judges and the noble-faced policemen whose words are the words of mathematical, steel-tipped, copper-bottomed truth, sadness steals over me at the sight of the unregenerate ruffians who get locked up. Still—still, there is a silver lining to the darkest cloud. For my sadness is mitigated when I think of the stout and handsome salaries that the lofty-browed judges receive for sentencing the locked-up ruffians to the punishments they so richly deserve.

Well do I know that there are wicked philosophers who say that judges and policemen are in the essence no better than the ruffians they either lock up or sentence. And when I think of these wicked philosophers it gives me the shivers. For I earn a bit now and then by doing a bit of philosophy myself, and I wouldn't like anyone to think that I was even distantly related in color of thought to the philosophers who have the cheek to say that judges and policemen are not the noblest people that ever happened.

The morality that guides the State is somewhat different from the morality that guides the individual. It moves on what you might call broad and easy lines. There is nothing narrow about it. It is a free-and-easy, heads-I-win-tails-you-lose kind of morality.

It bends in all directions, and still there is a simplicity and directness about it that you are bound to admire. If the State wants a thing, it takes it.

The morality of the State was invented by the genius to whom the idea occurred that it would be a fine thing if he could only get people to believe that no one had a right to kill and steal but himself. This genius of old saw that if he inoculated people with this idea, he and his descendants could enjoy the fruits of his labors with security and case.

Such undoubtedly must have been the genesis of the morality of the State. You were to be the good, nice, pious, turn-the-other-cheek kind of person, whilst I was the bold, daring, sufficient-unto-himself-take-everything-in-sight kind of person.

Like all really great inventions the invention of the morality of the State was simplicity itself. Or rather, it seemed simple after it was invented.

Before this morality came into being, everybody felt that he had as much right to kill and steal as his neighbor. And rows were going through the whole of the time.

And lo! there came upon the scene the Benefactor, who stole all that was stealable, and then laid down the rule that no one was to kill or steal but himself.

I can picture this primeval statesman telling the people whom he had knocked about—and from whom he had stolen everything—how nice it would be if they stopped fighting and stealing. I can feel the pathos in his voice and I can see the noble and beatific expression of his face as he told his listeners how good and kind he was. I can hear him laying down the morality that was destined to guide the great empires to come. I can see his club falling with convincing effect upon the sconce of the one who had not the wit to grasp the beauty of his spoken argument.

Ideas give birth to ideas. And out of the first idea grew another. It occurred to our dear old skull-cracking, primeval statesman that it would be a finer thing yet to catch people young and inoculate them with the nobility and beauty of the idea of letting other people do all the stealing and killing.

In a word, our primeval skull-cracker invented the copybook maxim. And he went even further. He invented the Church. The youth of that interesting epoch were not only taught that it was a noble and beautiful thing to let other people have everything worth having. They were also taught that it was a holy and edifying thing.

How strange are the beginnings of things. We owe the beauty and grandeur and magnificence and pomp and holiness and sacredness and idealism of the State and the Church to a club.

And whenever I go to Westminster and gaze upon the huge, artistically ornamented, and beautifully gilded club, that reposes before the Speaker in the chamber where orators orate for the welfare of dear old England, my mind travels back to the good old primal statesman. I think of the debt we owe to the sturdy inventor of the State and the Church, and State morality.

He builded better than he knew.

Whilst the two moralities—the morality that guides the State, and the morality that guides the individual—are quite different, still, they are the same. In this sense, I mean. One could not exist without the other. They fit exactly into each other. They are as nearly related as the head is to the body.

If the individual were to take for his guidance the morality that guides the State, the State would have to go out of business. It would have to put up the shutters.

But fortunately, there is very little fear of such an awful thing as this happening. For there are in the world such places as Exeter Hall. In places such as this the beautiful turn-the-other-cheek philosophy is still taught. We have also philosophers like the calm and lofty Tolstoy who advises men to take kicks lying down. The theory of the calm and lofty Russian philosopher is that when the kicker is so tired of kicking you that he can't kick you any more, he will stop. Which is true enough.

The Exeter Hall-cum-Tolstoy philosophy fits in as naturally into the Grand Duke-cum-Cossack philosophy as an animal fits into its skin. And therefore is it that the calm and idyllic Tolstoy is never bothered. Nobody thinks of locking him up. And I can only say that I thoroughly agree with the Grand Ducal attitude towards the bewhiskered apostle of peace. Indeed, were I a Grand Duke, I would take good old Tolstoy by the hand.

And so it goes throughout the whole of the world. The turn-the-other-cheek and the might-is-right philosophies are in reality one and indivisible.

And here I must finish this illuminating study. And I hope that the point I have made is quite clear to you all: that the two moralities—the morality that guides the State, and the morality that guides the individual—had a common source.

I hope that I have made it clear that they were invented at one and the same moment by the skull-cracking statesman who led a gay and interesting life in the fine old merry times of old!

ONE OF MAN'S COMIC QUALITIES is shown in the way he will gravely reason about a thing that is absurd on the face of it. Lengthy argument will be gone into concerning propositions which would not bother the mind of a four-year-old child for a moment.

It pains me to have to say what I am going to say, for I revere the race of beings to whom I have the honor of belonging with the strongest and most powerful kind of a reverence. But a fact is a fact. And the fact is that men get more stupid as they grow older. The human being starts with a good, bright mind. As everyone knows, children are famous for their straight and apt and acute way of viewing things. But the child's mind is soon, alas! dulled by the process that is called education. Schools and colleges and other brain-benumbing institutions kill the mother-wit that the human being began with. And by the time the human being is fully developed, physically, he is a fool altogether.

I trust it will not be thought by my fellow-men that I put on record the above fact meaning to be in any way sharp or severe. For I like men. They are very good fellows indeed. Their trust in each other is enormous. If you disbelieve this assertion, go into the City and promote a company. You will then find that man's trust in man is not only fathomless. It is immeasurable. Yes, our good, dear old friend, man, is—in the hoodwinkable sense—absolutely the easiest proposition of all the races of animals. And I, therefore, haste to render an apology for all the rude and hard things that have ever been put forth by my more or less gifted brothers of the pen. Man is the most simple and likable of the world's innumerable races of beings. And his comic way of reasoning around absurd propositions makes the truly sympathetic thinker only like him all the more.

Take the evergreen proposition about land. Men say that they own land. Why they say so is too deep for my intellect to fathom. But they say it, nevertheless. And lo! giants of intellect arise who assert that it is impossible to own land.

And they preach against the sin of men owning vast domains. And these giants of intellect often enough write long and wildly thrilling books which prove on sound economic lines that owning land is wrong.

In view of the fact that you can't carry a wide and vast domain around in your breeches pocket, it seems to me that the writing of a long and wildly thrilling book concerning so self-evident a fact is a waste of good ink and paper. And I have often wondered why these famous writers on economics did not bend their energies in the direction of writing detective stories, or love stories with happy endings. Their literary gift would then have served some really useful purpose. But writing a book which puts forth in a long, dull, and grave manner the fact that a man cannot own land is like putting forth a book which would tell you that you can't jump to the moon, or sail a battleship to Mars.

We all know that you can't own land. Indeed, this fact has been as plain as the nose on your face through the whole of the hundreds of thousands of years that man has honored this planet with his presence. And not only can you not own land. You can't even steal it. You can no more steal and carry it off than you can steal and carry off the air or the ocean. I would like to see a victorious army carrying off even a field in their knapsacks. The utmost you can do is to knock the people on the head who have enough sense of humor to say that they own the land.

And when you have done that you may steal the joke of the departed humorist. But that is all you can steal. Just the joke. And the land will be there even after some other humorist has come and knocked you on the head and stolen the joke that you stole.

To a four-year-old child all this would be very plain. But to the man it is not plain at all. He sees in it curiously involved issues that must be carefully and cautiously dealt with. And so he writes books about it, or he makes speeches in Parliament about it, or he growls about it over his beer.

Men also reason in the same absurd way about killing men. To kill a man is on the face of it an act of rudeness. People don't like to be killed, and they have made laws calculated to discourage such acts. Some two thousand years ago in England a man was what you might call his own guide, philosopher and friend. He was his own lawyer and judge and jury and executioner. It is not for me to say that the responsibility of having to be all these things did not confer some advantages upon the simple men of old. Indeed, I should think that it forced the ancient Englishman to be a rather watchful, help-yourself kind of person. The kind of man it was just as well not to slap upon the back without an introduction. But let us to the point.

At present it is not considered quite the thing to go around killing people. But if the people—who honor you by making a handsome thing out of ruling you—get vexed, they can suddenly turn killing into the highest kind of a virtue. They will clap a uniform on to your back and send you out with bands of other uniformed persons to kill as many people as you possibly can. I am not, of course, saying that war is not justified. I would not have the courage to put forward so dreadful a heresy. As everyone knows, wars are always inevitable. I am only pointing out how curiously man reasons about the killing of man. The same thing is at once a crime and a virtue.

One might think that to kill a man was to kill a man. But such is not the case. Or rather I mean to say that there are times when absolutely the same thing is a different thing altogether.

The reason, of course, of this is— Well, it is not for me to attempt an explanation. I must refer you to the highly placed soldiers and statesmen and emperors and such like who earn honor and glory, and a living, by the keeping up of the dignity of their respective nations. They know all about it, and the man in the street knows all about it.

But to a donkey the reasoning of these intellectual people would seem a trifle odd.

However, it is not for me to say anything invidious concerning the race of beings to which I belong. For it might be answered that whilst animals have more sense than man, they certainly do not possess man's sense of humor. True! The subtle comedy of paying rent to a man, who said he owned the land, would be of too airy and elusive a nature for the intellect of the donkey to grasp. And if ten donkeys were to go into a rich field of grass and one of them told the other nine that they were only to take a mouthful now and then whilst he grazed at his will and pleasure—I fear that no paper would dare to print the language of the other nine donkeys. I mean were such language translatable.

I might go at length into man's humorous methods of reasoning. But charity and good feeling bid me refrain. For man is the best of fellows when you get to know him.

But where—oh, where did he get his intellect?

I AM TIRED OF HEARING the word "if" used when people are talking about machinery. For the word "if" is of all words the most dreadful. It is the spoiler and the disintegrator of all the beautiful, alleged philosophy that lies in the innumerable books that have been written by the world's innumerable thinkers. This word has exactly the opposite effect to the keystone in an arch. Introduce it into a scheme of argument or philosophy and it at once shatters and scatters it.

People say that machinery would be the finest blessing that has ever been inflicted upon this unfortunate world "if" people were grand and noble and disinterested beings. But when you are fronted with the fact that the world is not filled to the brim with grand and noble and disinterested beings, you can only wonder why people of alleged intelligence waste their breath and their time and your time in telling you what would happen were white-winged angels honoring the world by populating it. You have got to take the world as you find it whether you like it or not. This is what the person who is reckoned to be a common or garden blockhead does. And my study of life has forced me to the conclusion that quite often the uneducated or common or garden blockhead knows more than many a famous philosopher who has embalmed his unworkable theories in books.

The fact of the matter is that machinery, as I have often pointed out, has inflicted immense harm upon practically all the people of the nations that have adopted it. It ought not to be so, and if these said nations were inhabited by white-winged angels it very likely would not be so. But the fact remains. And you can no more argue the fact away than you can argue the sun and the moon away. Machinery is an utter curse to humanity.

Of course, there is a reason for this. And the reason that is given forth is that men are callous ruffians. What a callous ruffian may quite mean, I don't know. But I believe that when people use the term—in reference to the way men take advantage of machinery to oppress other men—they mean that a callous ruffian is a person who is out for the success of his own hand. Could angels get a hold of these wonderful, labor-saving appliances, say these people, in effect, all would— But we won't go into that again.

The truth of the matter is that the wonderful labor-saving appliance invariably gets into the hands of the callous ruffian who makes an immense amount of money and winds up by buying a shining title of honor and glory from a pleased and grateful State.

Whether these callous ruffians are an especial breed of men or not, I don't know. But I have a suspicion that noble people like you or me, gentle reader, would not wave away too hastily fifty thousand of the best per year just because it was got out of machines which the law of the land kindly allowed us to own.

Whilst I think of it just let me put in a word about rich men. Rich men undoubtedly should be abolished. And they will be abolished. But for all that there is a good deal of cant afloat concerning them.

The truth is that practically every human being wants to be rich. And rich men are simply a growth out of the ideal of the mass. When human beings no longer have the ideal of being rich, rich men will take upon themselves wings and fly off to some other more stupid world. The fault lies not in the rich, but in ourselves.

To return to machinery: It is a fact that men who labor with the hands have invariably opposed its introduction amongst them. And there has been the usual indignation expressed by the philanthropic sweaters whose ideal it was to get the noblest kind of a living out of the labor of other people. These philanthropic sweaters were naturally put about when mere workingmen grumbled because their living was done away with. The argument of the philanthropic sweater was that these vulgar work-people ought to allow their families to starve so that genius in the shape of making labor-saving appliances could have its fling. "Ah," the philanthropic sweater would say, "it is true that you and your families will starve, but be disinterested and console yourself with the idea that men far away will be able to keep themselves and their families by the making of the beautiful machines. Be Christian. Be charitable. Above all, be noble."

Men who labor may be thick-headed. Indeed, I will assert positively that they are thick-headed. But however thick your head may be, you will feel the discomfort of being hungry and having no place to sleep. And however dull you may be, it will rouse you to fire when your children cry for bread. And it takes no University training to enable you to feel the insult and the sneer that lies behind the words of the man who tells you to console yourself with the idea that men far away are doing very well at your expense.

Besides, working-men are not so dull as they appear after all. Their judgment about life is sounder than the judgment of men who get fancy educations. For it is formed on a first-hand knowledge of fact. And this is the only way that any judgment that is worth anything can be formed.

Working-men have always been against the introduction of machinery. For they knew that it would be used against them. They knew that machinery was a weapon introduced for their destruction. And naturally they were against it.

But there is a stronger case against machinery even than that that is contained in the fact that it causes working-men and their families to starve.

The strongest case of all against machinery is that the use of it degrades and takes the power out of human beings. It stops the growth of men in every way. Through machinery men become less men both mentally and physically. Individuality is destroyed. And the nation that takes up machinery is doomed and damned in the end. For the life and the power of the units of the nation is weakened. Besides, machinery is a destroyer of everything that is beautiful. See the way the horrible tram-machines have destroyed the beauty of the Embankment—one of the finest of the world's promenades.

And the introduction of machinery has been responsible for the insane rush of the people into great towns.

Machinery has introduced cowardice into the art of fighting. Men don't fight nowadays. They sneak behind rocks and take potshots at each other.

Of course, it will be said by thoughtless people that machinery has largely stopped the indiscriminate hand-to-hand fighting that used to go on in the good old barbarous days of old. It will be said that it has brought more peace into the world. So it has. But what sort of a peace? I will tell you. It has brought a peace that has more horror in it than the most savage and desolating of the old-fashioned raiding wars. In this charming peace human beings are more subjected and crushed than they were in the days when men used to look on war as a healthy exercise. Which it is. The very healthiest.

The mass of human beings were never in such subjection as they are in the midst of the security of the world's machine-ridden nations. In the days of old you went out armed, and you had to keep your weather eye open. But keeping your weather eye open made more of a man out of you.

Hard things were done in the old fighting days. But the horrible things never happened that happen now in the world's great towns. People were killed outright—decently. They were not sweated and starved to death in noisome dens by smooth, suave, machine-adoring philanthropists.

Machinery is a mistake. It is against the development of humanity. It is a turning back of the hands of the clock.

7

The Folly Of Thrift.

THE WORKING CLASSES WHO MAKE a bare exis-
tence are all the time being counselled to practice the virtue
of thrift.

Well-clad and well-housed and well-fed ministers of the Gospel
stand up in pulpits and deal forth words of unctuous wisdom to
the effect that the lower orders should economize on their beer and
tobacco and enjoyments generally.

These starvelings at the feast of life are adjured to save money
out of their low earnings. The lack of thrift of the working man!
This subject causes taps of various kinds of hypocritical eloquence
to flow. It is one of the favorite themes of the millionaire and the
statesman and the bishop. And I don't wonder.

Thrift supports millionaires. For the thrift of the lower orders is
the opportunity of these eloquent persons. But for that thrift—which
is a folly of the most foolish kind—the millionaire would be unable
to steal his millions, and the statesmen and bishops and others of
that useful ilk would be unable to revel luxuriously in their present
fat salaries.

Even I myself would lapse into flowing and dulcet periods of oratory concerning thrift were I a statesman or a bishop or a millionaire. I would blossom forth into a Demosthenes.

Here let me state a cold fact.

The wages of all people that work with the hands have an irresistible tendency to sink to a certain point. This point is represented by the standard of comfort at which the worker can, or is satisfied to, live. I wish to make this as clear as I can, for it is the crux of the whole subject.

If you are a coolie[17] who lives upon rice, and wears little more than a loincloth, your wages will be at the point where you can just buy the rice and the few slight coverings you need. Your wages will sink no lower than this point, for were it to do so you would sicken and die, and you would be no longer of use to your employer. And your wages will not rise above the living point, for there are plenty of other coolies who are satisfied to do your work for a bare living. You are kept exactly at the point where you are of the most use to your employer. You are allowed to live, and no more. You are getting what is called a living wage.

If, on the other hand, you are an English workman you will get just the amount of wages that will satisfy the general idea of living and comfort of men of your own class. Here there is not the absolute, ironclad definition of the wage point that there is in the case of the coolie, for Englishmen naturally wish to do better than to just get a bare living. Englishmen like to drink and to smoke and enjoy themselves. They refuse to live as the spiritless coolie lives. They try to keep up to a certain standard of comfort.

And so there comes to be a slight margin over after the actual life-wants of the Englishman are satisfied.

---

17 "coolie" is an offensive and derogatory word used primarily in the 19th century to describe and refer to low-paid laborers from Asia.

This margin the employer is always trying to steal. He is always endeavoring to force the Englishman into the position of the coolie, who is allowed to barely live and no more. I don't say that absolutely all employers are like this, but practically the universal tendency is to try and steal from the English worker the little margin that is left over from his wages after he has bought food for himself and his family.

One of the ways of doing this is to preach thrift to him. He is told to deny and stint himself so that he can save. And bishops and statesmen and others are turned loose upon him, for all these people are in league with his employers to rob him.

He saves, and what happens?

Why, the money is stolen from him in an underhand way. As soon as his landlord thinks he can stand it his rent is raised, or his wages are lowered by his employer. There comes into play the tendency to force wages down to the bare living point. There are many ways of stealing what he has saved, but this is the chief way. As a matter of fact, the people who preach thrift to him are not thrifty themselves. Almost all of them live fully up to their incomes, and many of them live past it.

Money is round and it was made to go round.

If everyone in the world were to hoard up their money business would come to a standstill.

The miser is a far greater danger to the State than a burglar.

Let us be just, however. Let us have fair play.

The people who so strenuously advise the working man to save up are not actuated with the spirit of the miser. They are jolly, whole-souled persons who want to get at and spend this thrift-gained money for themselves. They are the drones who hunger after the honey that the working bees have hoarded.

In a sort of way I admire them. They are sharp persons who have solved the deep problem of living dishonestly without getting into jail.

Thrift is against the law of nature. Nature is profuse and open-handed and lavish. She spends everything she has without fear or thought of the morrow.

Thrift is at best but a cowardly virtue. And a cowardly virtue is far more criminal than a good, healthy, open-and-above-board vice.

Working men! Pay no attention to these fellows who preach thrift to you. Remember that they are jokers. Jokers of talent, of course, but still jokers. Spend your bit while you have a chance. It is a poor heart that never rejoices. And also remember that the time will come into the world when things will be made better for you. But it will not come by the way of hoarding up your earnings, so that sharp men who don't work can collar them. It will only come by your demanding more than you have at present.

Beware of thrift!

8

Lending And Borrowing.

BORROWING IS THE MOST ANCIENT of the fine arts.

It undoubtedly began with some prehistoric genius, who, realizing that he could not get what he wanted by the simpler methods of force, had recourse to persuasive methods that were soothing and subtle. He told the man whom he wished to borrow from things that pleased this man. In my mind's eye I can see the hard face of our rude, borrowing forefather softening as he enlarged upon the virtues of the person from whom he wished to borrow a flint or club or other belonging. I can almost hear his rough speech as it clothed itself with its first real grace.

Such undoubtedly was the beginning of the noble art of borrowing.

And it is not too much to say that humanity owes the deepest kind of debt to this prehistoric, borrowing genius. For he was the first to see that intelligent and soothing persuasion might possibly be a mightier weapon than the club. He was the primal diplomat. He was the first worker upon that variable and complex quantity that is called human nature. He introduced politeness into a world of rudeness.

All hail to the first borrower.

THERE ARE SHALLOW PEOPLE WHO imagine that Shakespeare was against borrowing because of the words he put into the mouth of Polonius. But these people are surely wrong. For the great Shakespeare must have been a skillful borrower himself in the days before his plays had vogue. And besides, he holds Polonius up to ridicule, and makes him come to an unfortunate end. I don't know of course what was in Shakespeare's mind when he was drawing this character, but I would lay a pound to a penny that the foolish speech concerning borrowing and lending which he put into the mouth of Polonius was intended but to set off the utter foolishness and ineptness of this character.

Though hard-hearted and skinflint people will scarcely credit it, there are in this cold world people who really like to lend money. I don't mean the money-lending harpies who exact all kinds of interest. I mean that there are people who really like obliging other people with loans, and who are very pleased if they get back the bare amount they lent. They will lend a friend or an acquaintance money on no other security than the understanding that they will get it back at some indefinite period. And when they lend this money, they feel a positive thrill of enjoyment.

Such people are truly the salt of the earth.

When you are in a hole or a difficulty, all you have to do is to go to them and they will pull you out. And so pleased are they at being able to help you that they will like as not stand you a dinner as a kind of perquisite for your allowing them to help you.

These noble souls exist in the world. I know, for I have met them. And when I am at my favorite game of railing at the world, I often pause, conscience stricken, when I think of them. For the world, when it produces such people, can't be such a bad old world after all.

Mind you, they are not charitable people. I would not insult them by comparing them to charitable people. For charitable people are usually people who give money—that they have never earned from a lofty height.

No, they are infinitely finer and better than charity mongers. For they will lend you a fiver or a tenner, and with the lending of it there will be no suggestion that they are in any way better than you are. They expect it back, when it is convenient for you to give it back. And so you feel no humiliation. You are as much a man as you were before you borrowed it.

When these people die, I am positively certain that they go straight to Heaven.

M IND YOU, YOU MUST UNDERSTAND THIS: You are expected to pay the money back. If you don't, your account with them is closed. You can never borrow from them again.

And were their attitude to be other than this, it would be bad for you. For then the money you got from them would have the debasing effect that money has when it is given in charity.

You must give it back.

I know what hard-fisted, skinflint people will say to all this. They will say that such a man loses the money he lends.

But such is not the case.

These generous lenders of money almost always get their money back. Rarely does it happen that they lose what they have lent. In ninety-nine cases out of a hundred the man who borrows from them pays up. If he does not pay up, it is because he is utterly unable to do so. And should a run of luck come to him in after years, he will pay up invariably.

For such a debt is in the truest and most real sense a debt of honor. Even the most unscrupulous man is apt to feel this.

A WORD AS TO THE AMOUNT that a man ought to borrow from the friend who takes pleasure in the lending of money: Never borrow small sums such as crowns or half-crowns. For these sums are liable to be forgotten. Always borrow an even sum, say, such as a sovereign, or a fiver, or a tenner. And when you are paying back the loan, pay back the whole of it in one sum.

This makes the transaction easier and simpler. If it is not convenient to pay the loan back within a reasonable time, it is better to wait than to pay it back in installments. The installment method is a nuisance to the man who has lent you the money, and besides, it gives to the whole transaction a business air that in no way belongs to it. It is simply an affair between friends. And always remember that even when you do pay back the sum you have borrowed, you are still in your friend's debt in a money sense. At least you would be in his debt were the transaction a business one, for money in itself earns interest.

Neither must you offer him security. For it is likely that your security would be but a one-legged security that would in no way stand in a business sense, and even were it gilt-edged it is suggesting that your friend is a professional moneylender when you offer it.

And don't specify the exact day or hour when you will pay it back. This is apt to throw your friend off.

Just borrow it in a swift, straightforward manner.

How thankful the generous lender of money is when the friend whom he has obliged pays him back. He feels a lifting of heart. A pleased look overspreads his face. In a way he feels as joyful as if he had found the money that his debtor has just given him. There are reasons for this. In the first place it is likely that though he wanted it back, in his heart of hearts he looked upon the money in a sense as lost when he lent it. He would not let the one whom he has obliged know of this feeling for worlds. Perhaps he would not even own to himself that he had it. But he must have it, or how would the look of surprised joy overspread his face when he is paid back? I have often observed this look. The lender's face becomes positively beautiful. And again he feels that his friend is a good and honorable fellow whom he can trust. He has got his money and his friend back again.

He feels joy, does this lender of money.

And I firmly believe that, were it possible he would reverse the financial law and pay his debtor interest on the money that he had been kind enough to borrow from him.

9

The Power Of Gold.

I T IS AGAINST THE LAW of change for the power of gold to remain as it is. And change is of all laws the law—if I may so phrase it—that is absolutely immutable. Change is the very condition and essence of being. A man is born, he lives, he dies, he is resolved again into the elements. Nations come and live and pass. It is not given that you may escape change.

And so it is that the power of gold must pass.

It is not for me to say that gold has not had its use in the world. But for it you could not have concentrated and marshalled the power of labor. You could not have carried into effect the world's vast engineering projects. Undoubtedly it has been of benefit to man in the sense of the linking up of the world's forces. Gold was a magical talisman that man obeyed. It stood as an ideal authority that none might question. It was at once mighty and potent and persuasive and subtle. It reached into all places. If it gained not its effect by direct means, it came indirectly. For were you one who would not obey the command of this magical talisman, there were others who would. Others upon whom you depended—or who affected you.

And so it came to pass that gold ruled the world.

And it is not to be said that its rule was in the essence a maleficent rule. For gold sent forth ships bearing wealth to exchange for wealth. Through gold the world became civilized. I am not one who holds that this gold-made civilization is a finer phase of social life than the savagery it displaced. But this may be said for it: It at least tends in the direction of the races of men coming to a common understanding.

And civilization arose and lived at the behest of the yellow, magical talisman. At the bidding of this wondrous god mighty cities came into being.

Gold controlled and guided human effort. It was the supreme autocrat.

This strange and wonderful gold! Where is the imagination that could conceive a romance such as the romance of its history and the workings of its complex and manifold power? What man of genius of the beginning could foresee the coming into the world of this power so immense and potent and all-reaching?

This genie mightier a million-fold than the genie of the Arab tales!

G OLD IS AUTHORITY.
And that authority in the end lives but for itself might be put forth as an axiom. I mean when authority has accomplished the end it set out to accomplish. No student of history or of life can deny this. Authority must inevitably come to the conclusion that the greatest good that can happen is that it remains forever in power.

At a certain stage when authority is disinterested it is a necessary thing in the ordering of affairs. There are times when it is vital that a leader be obeyed. The hero who is freeing his country from servitude must be loyally followed by those who would help him. There are times when you must obey, that is if you have agreed to obey.

The confusion that exists in the world as to the value of authority has arisen in this manner: Primarily, authority was but a means to an end. It was the most effective way of marshalling the forces at hand so that a given object could be accomplished. A strong and capable man, say, gathered the fighters from out his people and repelled an invasion. Men subjected their wills to him so that they might avoid destruction. They mortgaged their liberty for a period.

Thus was authority created. Not as an end in itself, but as an expedient for the gaining of an end.

You know the rest. When authority was put into power it—after a time—arrogated to itself the right to remain forever in power. And no crime was too terrible for it to commit so that it might remain in power. This is to be seen before our eyes at the present time. The governments whose authority is being questioned by the people are treating these people in a dreadful manner.

I deny neither the value of authority nor the respect that is owing to it. But I deny that authority has the right to exist in perpetuity.

Authority is but a means to an end.

And the ultimate and finest end of all is liberty. And when authority would seek to prevent man from gaining this end, authority must and will be destroyed.

It has come to pass that the power of gold holds the world in subjugation. It has usurped the power that once was held by fighting men. The real kings of the world are the men who hold it.

The necessity of commerce having a recognized unit, representing value, brought it into being. And it grew till it became the most stupendous power the world has known.

But its day is passing. Commerce has so grown that gold is unable to cope with the work that is put upon it as a medium of exchange. There is not enough of it. Sooner or later the nations must agree upon another unit that represents value.

When this comes to pass, the back of the power of gold will be broken. In fact the breaking of the power of gold will mean the destroying of the very principle that a unit—representing value—shall have any power at all.

When the principle, that the unit of value possesses power in itself, shall be destroyed, a great bar to liberty will be removed. Man will advance in wisdom. He will learn to be at once free as an individual and to have a sense of inter-relation with his fellow men.

There will be no such a thing as a unit expressing value. There will be but the value itself.

Which is labor.

THE TIME IS EVEN NOW coming when the gigantic debts that gold has forced upon the world will be repudiated.

If I were to tell you that your grandfather owed my grandfather ten thousand pounds and that you were to pay me interest upon that debt, you would laugh at it as a joke. And if you thought that I was really serious, you would look upon me as a lunatic.

Yet this foolish thing actually happens with nations. Our grandfathers and great-grandfathers and other ancestors borrowed money for all kinds of purposes, and these debts of theirs still hang as millstones around our necks. We have to pay interest on them. There is comedy in this whole matter—dearly bought comedy, but still comedy.

This foolish proceeding cannot, of course, last. Man may be many things, but he is not by nature an idiot.

Nations will repudiate these absurd things that are called national debts. Indeed, nations will have to do it whether they like it or not, for the strain that is put upon Labour to satisfy these unjust calls will in the end be too much.

Nations will become bankrupt. In fact it only requires one to become bankrupt for the rest to follow.

In that event, our creditors will have to go and dun our grandfathers and great-grandfathers and other ancestors in the realms where they are at present residing.

Let this be understood about gold: If you possess a hundred or a thousand or a million pounds, it does not mean that you possess so much value. It only means that you possess a call upon so much value. You simply possess the power to commandeer—the exact word—produce and labor to a specified extent. A Bank of England note is in no sense value. It is simply a piece of paper upon which is printed an order to get something of value. You may never have done a stroke of work in your life, and someone may have given you a million pounds. And you are therefore able to commandeer produce and labor to that extent.

The power of gold will pass. It has done its work, and who is there to say that it has not been amply recompensed for that work?

In fact it has become its own enemy. For not content with its power it has magnified it a million-fold. Gold acts as though it were incomparably bigger than it is. It has inflated itself almost beyond conception.

It has taken on a bigger load than it can carry.

10

Interest.

O NE OF THE REASONS WHY I like man so much is because of his simple and ingenious nature. And I am certainly not at one with those alleged philosophers who accuse him of being a dark, deep, double-dyed ruffian. He is neither dark nor deep nor wily. Indeed, he is in reality the simplest of all the animals. And it gives me pain to think that this beautiful quality has not been given emphasis by any more distinguished brothers of the pen.

Have you ever, my dear and gentle reader, thought anything about the law of interest? You must, of course—especially if you have ever had things in pawn. If you have never had anything in pawn, then at once accept my humble apology for even suggesting such a thing. But I have often left things with my Uncle, and therefore know a thing or two about the law of interest.

It is not my intention here to go into any involved, economic definition of this law, for the reason that my mind isn't heavy enough to understand economics.

Economics are too deep for me.

But I will consider the law in a simple, come-day, go-day way.

In the first place, let me express for the law of interest my heartiest and most unadulterated admiration. It is the finest and most beautiful law in the whole wide, wide world.

If you possess a big enough sum of money all you have to do is to sit back in your chair, smoke beautiful Havana cigars, and ponder upon the beauty of the world. You won't have to do a hand's turn. Everybody is only too anxious to work for you. The reason for this happy state of affairs is because you possess a certain amount of yellow metal.

Through the law of interest this metal will get you things without any bother. You can go off on long and joyous holidays, you can go and hear Caruso warbling divinely, you may dine where you will. All these things will be given without your doing a stroke of work.

I call it fine. And I am not at one with the sour curmudgeons who say that such a thing is wrong. I will frankly confess that I wish this law would do a bit for me. It would be great to be able to do nothing, and still to have everything. It would suit a thoughtful loafer like myself to a T.

But I wonder what would happen did an animal try on this interest business with his brother animals? Would all the lions hunt for another lion just because he possessed a dead lump of metal? Suppose a beaver possessed such a thing, would all the beavers beave for him? I wonder! Oh, I wonder!

Suppose a donkey proposed to the other donkeys that they should do his work on the strength of his having this same dead lump of metal. What do you think would happen? What do you think the other donkeys would say?

I fear, my dear and gentle reader, that the donkeys would bray forth a chorus of rude remarks.

The longer I live the more do I see that the animals know a thing or two. I fear that they are much shrewder than men suppose.

Of course, I know that the law of interest can be defended on the best of grounds. Of course, I know that it is as sound as the law of gravitation. If the law of interest were to fall in abeyance, our poor old earth would forget to revolve.

Knowing this, I do not dare to tilt at it. I would not make rude remarks about it for the world. For I am no donkey. I am a man, and I have therefore the deepest respect for this magical law.

W HEN I WAS A BOY I read of many strange and wonderful laws in the "Arabian Nights." All sorts of odd and strange things happened. A genie was worth having as a friend. He could put into force, for your benefit, mysterious agencies.

But I can think of no law or agency in the "Arabian Nights" so effective or so wonderful as the law of interest.

For by the law of interest gold grows, and still does not grow. It gets bigger, and still it remains the same size. A hundred thousand pounds will double itself in a comparatively few years, and still in actual size it is no more, not even by a half sovereign. It is as a tree that yields fruit, and still does not yield fruit. The fruit is actual. It is there. You can eat it. And still it is not on the tree. The tree never had the least thing to do with the fruit, and still it produces it.

But I won't go on with the Chinese puzzledom of this odd law. For whatever my crimes may be, I am not a writer on economics.

I will only remark that the law of gravitation, and the law of atomics, and the laws governing electricity, and all the laws known and unknown, suspected and unsuspected, are as nothing in their mysteriousness and power when compared with the law of interest. The law of interest could give all these laws cards and spades and beat them hands down.

Again do I say that it is a law for which I have the deepest respect. And did I possess the block of yellow metal necessary to set this law working on my behalf, I would not only not work—I would stop even writing about not working. Again would I go on tramp. But this time my tramping would be of the gilt-edged variety.

I WONDER WHO INVENTED THIS LAW. It surely could not have been man. For man is far too simple and ingenious an animal to ever have had the intellect to even dream of it.

The fact that some men benefit by the working of this super-magical law in no way proves that man invented it. As near as I can get at it, this law has always been in existence.

And I am led to the conclusion that some far wilier animal than man invented it. How this animal transmitted the idea to man I am not prepared to show. At least not in this present screed.

I WONDER WHAT THE PEOPLE of Mars will say about the matter when our astronomers have managed so that we can exchange gossip with them? Will they be able to tell us of a law of theirs that is half so curious and wonderful?

I doubt it. I doubt it very much indeed. I doubt if they possess a law that can make a thing at once grow and keep perfectly still, that, But I am forgetting. I went into all that a moment ago.

HOWEVER, I DO HOPE THAT the next great writer, the next Carlyle or Victor Hugo, will lay emphasis upon the ingenuous simplicity that forms so large an ingredient in the character of man. I do hope that he will bring into relief the fact that he possesses more innocence than all the animals put together. I hope that he will reveal man in his true character.

For I am tired of seeing man described as a dark, deep and scheming and wily ruffian.

The truth is that man is a being of the greenest and most verdant innocence. Politics alone might prove this.

But it is proved beyond all question by his reverence and respect for the law of interest.

Bart Kennedy
On Politics

Tramps sleeping on park bench, date unknown.

1

Shall Women Vote?

I T SADDENS ME TO THINK that women should be so
lost to all sense of what is proper and respectable as to go and
personally worry the mighty statesmen who orate in Westminster
for the general benefit of dear old England.

Ladies, you ought not to do it!

You ought to wait, as you have waited some hundreds of years,
till by the drip of time, so to speak, man's opposition to your voting
shall have worn away! With pain I have been reading of the way
you have actually gone and invaded the sacred halls of old, classic
Westminster. Demanding votes. It is dreadful. What would your
grandmothers have thought of all this?

And I, the merest of mere men, protest. You must refrain from
bothering these legislators. The poor men have enough to do, saving
England without being bothered in so preposterous a manner. Wait,
and it will be all right. Everything comes to him who waits, says the
dear old mossy proverb, *WAIT*.

Everything comes to him who will wait! This beautiful proverb
was doubtless invented by some humorist who had stolen everything

in sight, and who naturally desired that people should wait till he saw fit to give things back. "Wait." It is a good enough word, but it seems to me that "Take" is a better word.

But this is mere jest.

In all seriousness, I ask you, ladies, why you do not use constitutional means? Why don't you go about getting the vote in a proper and restrained and orderly manner? Don't mind the history books, for the history books say that governments never granted privileges to the governed save when the governed forced them. Always please remember that you are ladies.

And for Heaven's sake don't be misled by these history books. Read manuals on correct and nice and ladylike behavior.

And above all respect the sensitive feelings and tender consciences of politicians!

DO YOU KNOW THAT YOU are actually embarrassing these gentlemen by your goings on? Do you know that they don't like your way of coming into Westminster and ballyragging them? You disturb them as they are deeply pondering as to how they may become Cabinet ministers. You rudely break in on their dreams of drawing stout and handsome salaries.

It is not nice to do this. It is cruel. Oh, that I, a poor scribe, had but the power to properly depict the pain and embarrassment you cause.

Why, if you don't mind, you may actually help to cause the downfall of this present government.

Of course, we are comforted by the fact that a still nobler and more ideal band of politicians would then come to the fore. Finer and wiser and higher and purer beings would then orate and draw salaries for the benefit and honor and glory of the nation.

But even so. It is nonetheless cruel to do anything that might endanger the existence of the present Government. Be considerate of these statesmen. Some of them are not at all bad fellows.

Give 'em a chance.

REMEMBER THAT THE VOTE IS too sacred and potent a force to be lightly entrusted to anyone. If you were a statesman you would naturally be careful as to the selection of those to whom you gave the power and the privilege to elect you to a position of dignity and glory.

When you get the vote it will be all right. The world then would revolve the other way. The sun will shine every day. There will be no east winds.

See what the vote has done for the working man.

It will do as much for you, ladies.

BUT ENOUGH OF JOKING. In my opinion the vote is of no use at all. The history of politics shows that it has always been machined and captured for the benefit of the liars and tricksters who are classed under the generic name of politicians.

But that is no reason why women should not have the vote, if they want it. The average woman is at least as intelligent as the average man. And this is paying her but a poor compliment. And when men deny her the right to a voice in the ordering of public affairs they are simply guilty of impudent effrontery. Men at present have the running of public affairs, and who is there who has the assurance to say that women could possibly run them in a more stupid or corrupt way?

What man will deny that Europe at present is in a state of utter and stupid barbarism? No one knows the moment that a hideous and devastating war may break out. The men of Europe have not yet had the intelligence to devise a better means for the settling of disputes than that employed by the Hun, Attila.

It is just as bad in national and local affairs. Speaking, practically, the men who govern have no sense at all of the interests of those they govern. They just work blindly for their own personal interests. Their mouths, of course, are filled with fine and noble words. But they think only of themselves. The men who think otherwise are so few that they don't count.

I said a moment ago that I did not believe the vote was of use at all. And my reason for saying this is because man has not benefited by it. For years I lived in a country where manhood suffrage[18] was obtained in its broadest sense, and the practical result was that this very manhood suffrage was used to further oppress the masses. Because of the vote the masses were tricked by the politicians into thinking that they had some control over public affairs. And they therefore put up with injustices that they would never dream of putting up with were the government an absolute autocracy.

At present the vote is an utterly worthless thing. It is machined for the benefit of corrupt political cliques in the countries where it exists.

But how am I to know that the vote might not be of some use were it in the hands of women conjointly with men? Might not women bring a saner and nobler influence into politics? At any rate politics could sink no lower than they have sunk at present. They could be no more dangerous or corrupt.

---

18   "Manhood suffrage" was the 18th-century phrase used to describe the concept of "one man-one vote." During the European intellectual revolution of the late 1700s, there was a movement to bring democratic reforms to governmental systems that recognized the autonomy of individuals and that human beings deserved individual rights. (Of course, this was limited to only white men until the 20th century.)

It takes the man and the woman conjointly to make a whole human being. And no one can convince me that the counsel of women would not be of use in State affairs. The counsel of a woman is of value in the affairs of the family. Why not then in the State? The family was the genesis of the State. And the trouble and wrong that occur in the State are caused by its departure from the family ideal.

The only real objection that is adduced by men against women being allowed the vote is that they are not fitted to bear arms and to fight in the field. But even this objection has been disproved by history. Women can be trained as soldiers, and they have been proved to be as valuable as men in the field. In wild, frontier places, mothers have been as effective as fathers in the fighting for the defense of the home. They have been as brave and as skillful in the handling of weapons.

If women want the vote they must have it. It might bring the vote back into some repute.

At present the laws of all States treat women in a grossly unfair and mean way. This boasted chivalry business is the biggest hypocrisy of which man is guilty.

I am sorry, however, to be forced to say that some women are treacherous towards women. I mean the women who work against the suffrage movement. These are the most dangerous foes that have to be faced. They are slaves with the instinct of slaves, however clever they may be. And even though they may be unconscious of it, they act as they do simply to find favor with their masters, the men.

Go on, women. Get the vote. You might do some good. And I am glad to see that you have at last adopted the only means of getting it.

Which is to fight!

2

On Russia.[*]

EVEN PETER THE GREAT would not have been able to handle the present situation in Russia. He was a strong man, but there are times when individuals do not count. The most effective man is only effective when his ideas coincide with the ideas of others. In a word, what is called a great personality is but a man who is the mouthpiece or the carrier-out of the will of the crowd. When this concrete will becomes intense enough the man is found.

Napoleon said that he could have stopped the French Revolution. But the saying of this was only a boast. For Napoleon could no more have stayed the French Revolution than he could have stayed the rising of the tide with his bare hands. Mighty and effective though he was, he was cast aside the moment he got out of touch with his masters—the crowd. For let it never be forgotten that the world is not for a man or a few men. The world is for the multitude that dwell upon it.

All leaders fall when their egotism gets them out of touch with the masses who use them.

[*] January 29, 1905

This is the point: Does Russia want revolution? Do the whole people unitedly wish for change? If they do there will come forward the few resolute expressers of this united will. And Russia will emerge radiant from the bath of blood.

Before there are captains there must be fighting men.

Deny it who may, the present system of government in Russia arises out of and expresses the character of the people as a whole. No Government in the world would last for an hour were it not in accord with the will of the people. I mean in accord with the will of the people as a whole. It is not enough that a section of the people be discontented. The whole or the greater part of them must be ready for the change.

If you would light a fire, the fuel must be dry.

I have no hesitation in asserting that it is impossible for us here in England to have any real understanding of the situation in Russia. Great and powerful and skillful though the Press be, it is still incapable of performing the impossible feat of picturing with absolute fidelity the whole state of affairs. It can only tell us, so to speak, of the outside of events.

It is foolish and idle to blame the unlucky Czar. What can the man do? What could even the greatest or the strongest man do? A man, who is said to be strong, has control of the situation now, and what is he doing? He is helping on the discontent. He is making the fire greater.

Should revolution occur in Russia, it will be largely through Vladimir [Lenin]. This man of power and decision has in effect thrown his lot on the side of the terrorists who would rend the constitution from end to end. He has become the ally of the bomb-throwers and the secret and sudden users of the knife. His energy is devoted to the scuttling of the ship.

It is said that the Czar is afraid. Men sit in safe places and calmly criticize a man who is in one of the most terrible positions it is possible for a human being to be in. He is bound and helpless in the middle of a great fire, and he is expected to put it out.

The Czar might well be afraid. He is face to face with assassination through the day and through the night. It is a frightful thing this constant menace of assassination. It made even the iron Cromwell afraid.

The best thing that the Czar could do would be to leave Russia and let Vladimir carry out his rôle of unconscious arch-Nihilist. If the Czar stays he will be killed, and I firmly believe that the bureaucrats would kill him as quickly as the terrorists. Indeed, of the two I should think that the bureaucrats would show him the least mercy. They were most likely at the bottom of the last attempt upon his life.

It is well to remember that there are other countries where the soldiers would be bid to fire upon the masses who had come to demand their rights as men and human beings. The temper of all Governments is in the essential the same as the temper of the Russian Government. Russia alone has dared to go the whole length.

It is the insolence and iniquity of government by armed might that is on its trial. And men all over the world may take the lesson of Russia to heart. Englishmen may take it to heart as well as any other men.

The people who really precipitated the bloodshed in St. Petersburg were people of the trading class. These sweaters of the people would not allow their workmen even to put their grievances before them. And so there came the horrible bloodshed. It would be well if Vladimir turned his Cossack assassins upon these sweaters of the people.

And in England of the present day there are sweaters of the workers who are as the sweaters of St. Petersburg. The trading class has always been the sinister, disruptive element that in the end has destroyed Governments. They are traitors both to the ruling classes and the lower orders whose faces they grind. They upset the equilibrium between the governing and the governed. And we have plenty of instances of wretches of this class in the England of today men who would sell and are selling England.

The Russians will now see that their only remedy is to fight, if they really wish for a change. The philosophy of Tolstoy has been tried and found wanting.

And still the whole question of a revolution is so complex. The difficulty is not in the form of government that has to be removed. It is in human nature. Men are so easily divided into groups and classes. And men are affected by oaths and signs and symbols.

Soldiers will shoot down their brothers who are demanding liberty for themselves and the soldiers who are shooting them. These soldiers act in accordance with an unrighteous and treacherous oath.

These Cossack murderers, who have been tried in the field and found wanting, are slaves, as all soldiers are slaves. The unarmed people whom they shot down were fighting for their liberty as well as their own.

It may as well be said here that these Cossacks run away from the Japanese. They are of no account against armed men. Their only use is to kill unarmed people. They are expert at burning defenseless villages and slaying women and children. But all that they have shown in the field to the Japanese is the white feather. The bubble is pricked concerning their fighting qualities. They are exposed as a badly organized lot of savages, who are dangerous to everyone but the enemy.

In a revolution the soldier is the difficulty that has to be overcome. His training and surroundings are calculated to make a machine out of him. His power of thought is not developed. And the State, while it is using him, sees to it that he does not suffer as his brothers who are not soldiers often have to suffer. And so he is ready to kill at the word of command from his officer, who is for the most part a greater fool than he is.

Soldiers all over the world are like this even to such paragons as English soldiers.

There is also another element in the soldier question. When men are continually kept together and trained together for the purpose of killing, and are used to the having of deadly weapons in their hands, they are apt to feel a wish to use them. They are easily apt to feel that other people who are not soldiers are their enemies, even though these people are unarmed and are of their own race, and are asking for a common liberty for them all.

And they are apt to kill their brothers because they have taken an unrighteous and treacherous oath.

3

Votes And Vote-Catchers.

A S THINGS ARE AT PRESENT the power of the vote
is a myth and a delusion.

A man knows enough to get his daily bread, and that is enough
for him. The immense task of administering the nation's affairs he
leaves naturally to those who make a profession of it—the politicians.
These politicians give themselves such names as Tory Candidate,
or Liberal Candidate, or Labour Candidate, or Socialist Candidate.
And at elections they come and tell the man, whose time is taken
up earning his daily bread, how much they will do for him if he will
only exercise his Heaven-given privilege of voting for them.

The Tory will watch out for the honor of old England, the Liberal
will do the same in a subtly different manner, the Labourite talks in
a way at once vague and vehement of his own shining virtues when
compared to the awful vices of both Liberals and Tories, and the
Socialist threatens to inflict upon all men, high or low, the dread
and primal curse of work.

And so the man who possesses the Heaven-given privilege of
voting gets a trifle mixed and finally he votes for one or other of

these benefactors who come so nobly forward at election times, to thrust their benefactions upon him.

I may say here that there are some voters who demand a little spot cash from the two old, and, to my mind, over-condemned political parties. And I must also say that the Socialist and the Labourite are somewhat too fond of throwing stones at their brother politicians, the Liberal and Tory.

The Socialist and Labourite will indignantly deny that they are in any way related to these scoundrels, Mr. Liberal and Mr. Tory, and I therefore ask them this simple question: Do you not offer to give yourselves and your energies for the noble and beatific purpose of managing England's affairs for England's good? "Of course we do!" I can hear the powerful, electioneering voices of Mr. Socialist and Mr. Labourite shouting this answer to my question.

Right, oh, gentlemen. Right! And may I also say that the two people you abuse so much are out for the doing of the same thing. They have been found out, you answer. Aye, my lads, and so will you fellows be found out.

I said that there were some cynical voters who demanded a little spot cash from Mr. Liberal and Mr. Tory. But I am sorry now that I said this, for those who have to pay this spot cash don't like it mentioned.

Mr. Liberal and Mr. Tory don't mind paying hundreds of pounds in ways legitimate and legal for their seats, but the modest half-crown tipped into the horny palm of the exerciser of the Heaven-given privilege of— Ah! Silence! Hush! Don't mention it. You might get the man out of his seat.

Still, let us have fair does, as the vulgar saying puts it. It seems to me only fair that if Mr. Liberal and Mr. Tory have to tip the horny-handed son of toil a modest half-crown so that he of the horny hand will exercise his Heaven-given privilege of—well, why shouldn't Mr. Socialist and Mr. Labourite have to do the same thing?

For are not the whole of these four gentlemen out for the governing of England for England's good. Mr. Socialist and Mr. Labourite haven't the money, you say. And besides, Mr. Socialist and Mr. Labourite are beings of a far nobler and more disinterested cast than Mr.— Ah, stop it now. No throwing of stones. I'll take what you said about them not having the money. That is sufficient answer. You can't get blood from a stone.

But all I can say is that I don't think my friends Mr. Liberal and Mr. Tory are treated quite right by those base, horny-upturned-palmed gentlemen who ought to esteem it an honor to exercise their Heaven-given privilege for nothing I mean the privilege of putting noble and disinterested men into Parliament for the purpose of running good old England for good old England's good.

However— well, let that pass. And I may say that I'm sorry for mentioning it. Besides, I hear that the horny-handed person is getting ashamed of himself. He is beginning to feel the beauty and nobility of voting according to conscience.

And now I must do a thing that makes me tremble. I must call the much-abused Count de Witte[19] to my aid. He has enough on his shoulders already without my bothering him, for he has to deal with a host of people who are clamoring for the lofty and glorious privilege, which our horny-handed English ruffian now and then parts with for a modest half-crown. But I must call him to my aid.

---

19 Count Sergei Yulyevich Witte (June 29, 1849 – March 13, 1915) was a highly influential econometrician, minister, and prime minister in Imperial Russia, one of the key figures in the political arena at the end of the 19th and at the beginning of the 20th century.

Witte served under the last two emperors of Russia, Alexander III and Nicholas II. As Minister of Finance, Witte presided over extensive industrialization and the management of various railroad lines. He framed the October Manifesto of 1905, and the accompanying government communication, but was not convinced it would solve Russia's problem with the Tsarist autocracy.

On October 23, 1905 he became the first Chairman of the Russian Council of Ministers (Prime Minister). Assisted by his Council he designed Russia's first constitution. Within a few months, he fell into disgrace within court circles as a reformer. He resigned before the First Duma assembled. Witte was fully confident that he had resolved the main problem—providing political stability to the regime—but according to him the "peasant problem" would further determine the character of the Duma's activity.

He said a thing that was as true as that the wind blows and that the sun shines. He was talking to the people who were demanding manhood suffrage, and he said that in the United States—where the people had the blessing of manhood suffrage—the whole political power was bought by a few people. He said that manhood suffrage meant nothing. It is a terrible thing for a person like myself to have to quote on my behalf a pillar and a prop of the Russian Government.

But truth is truth even if the Devil spoke it.

And Count de Witte spoke nothing but the absolute and exact truth when he spoke to the effect that the vote in America was only a blind to gull the people.

I have lived for years in America, and I can bear witness to the truth of the Russian minister's saying. Manhood suffrage in America means less than nothing. The vote is bought and sold like any other piece of saleable merchandise. There are, of course, a few people who vote in accordance with what they fondly imagine to be their minds, but, in practice, the whole voting power of America is bought. Manhood suffrage means less than nothing, and no honest American will deny the truth of Count de Witte's assertion.

Ah, but we are so pure in England! We are too honest, and high-principled, and virtuous to do anything like that. Yes, of course, we own all the virtue of the world. We are the finest and purest and fairest and noblest people that ever happened. Who would not be an Englishman, when to be an Englishman means that you have all the planetary virtues rolled up in you? I am so glad to be an Englishman, and I only mention about this awful business of manhood suffrage being bought and sold so that America may see this illuminating screed on the power of the vote, and, seeing it, reform. Copy us, America, and you will be all right!

Be like us. Only vote so that noble and disinterested persons may rule America for America's good. And on second thoughts I take back what I said about manhood suffrage. And I'm sorry now for quoting Count de Witte.

Manhood suffrage would be all right did everybody vote for the noble and disinterested patriot.

Shade of Dr. Johnson! Avaunt!

I began this illuminating paper by an assertion that I really only meant as a joke. I said that as things are at present the power of the vote is a myth and a delusion. But, as I tell you, I did not mean it, for how could it be so, when the vote is a thing of such great and splendid power. Only for the vote you would be unable to put the patriot where he can do the most good. So I hope I have not given offence by anything I may have said.

Vote early, and vote often.

ONE OF THE THINGS THAT the men who represent labor must learn is not to be rude to the mere people outside.

I don't mean that they must wear top hats and black frock coats in Parliament, or that they must ape men who are called gentlemen. Neither must they refrain from giving hard knocks in the Council Chamber.

I mean that they must realize that they are not the only people on the earth, and that they by no means represent the last word that is to be spoken in the cause of progress.

Personally, I am in no way particularly enchanted or elated by the return of so many working-men to Parliament. If six hundred and seventy working-men were returned to Parliament the present evils would in time reproduce themselves. They would become as arrogant and as impudent as the men who rule England now. They would become a wire-pulling clique who had acquired the knack of perpetually keeping themselves in office.

The world suffers from the arrogance and impudence of the people who govern, and arrogance and impudence is just as insufferable from people in corduroys as from titled or wealthy people in top hat and frock coats.

People run away with the idea that the men who are sent to Parliament by the workers represent the best thought and power of the workers. Never was there such a delusion. The men who get to the top amongst working-men are mainly pushful spouters. They are glib, wordful fellows who don't like work. For which I would be the last to blame them. They share this dislike for work with lords and dukes and baronets. When I say that they don't like work, I mean, of course, that they don't want to do any real, useful, monotonous work. I, myself, who am a lazy indolent man, don't mind doing work that is interesting or exciting—especially if I am better paid for it than I would be for honest, useful labor.

I don't want working-men to become intoxicated and think that they are angels just because they have turned over in their dead sleep of centuries. They are no more angels than are dukes or baronets or lords or landlords. Indeed, some of these lords, working-men, etc., are a great deal better fellows than the best.

But my main point is that the men who represent labor must not be rude. That they are rude and arrogant everyone knows who has ever had the slightest thing to do with them. Labor leaders are the most impudent men under the sun.

Listen, my good lads who possess the gift of the gab! The world is a hoary old world, and your kind has appeared on the horizon before. And precious little you have done. So keep to the old size of your hats. You are by no means the pick of the working class. You are simply the trickiest of the working class. I can afford to say this, because I come from where you come from myself. I was like you. I was tricky enough to get out of the doing of real work. Kind may talk to kind, and therefore I tell you not to take yourselves too seriously. And above all stop being arrogant and rude.

For that is exactly the crime we have been grumbling about all these years and years. We are tired of the impudence of lords and dukes and successful, short-weight shopkeepers. And we don't want your impudence.

Try to be courteous. Try to realize that bossing other people is, even at its highest, but a necessary evil. Try to realize that we must somehow manage to live here together in England.

You must neither be rude to mere people outside, nor must you weaken when slapped on the back by a lord. You must, if possible, become your ideal. courteous men of sense. Anyway, let this be

It is a very good thing that you have been sent to Westminster—for yourself. But is it a very good thing for the people who have sent you to it? Is it?

You must understand that the people you represent are by no means the cream of the earth that is, if you take them by and large. But you know more about that than I can tell you. I, personally, would rather be a cart-horse than go to Westminster and have to depend for a living upon working-men. I don't know how you feel about it, but that's the way I feel. Working-men have been slaves too long to be nice people to work for. A few of them are all right, but only a few.

It is no good to do away with our present ruling experts if we are to have other ruling experts to take their place. I would as like have the old man of the sea that I have already on my back than change him for another. And here I must quote this Irish proverb: "It is better to have the divil you know than the divil you don't know."

I know what your ideal is, you labour members. I see it sticking out beneath your big words. Your ideal is exactly the same as the Liberal and Tory ideal. It is to make people, other than yourselves, work. Come on, now. Be frank. Isn't that your ideal? Don't you feel that you are perfectly capable of administering the affairs of this great country? You do, of course. You feel that you will do more good in Westminster than you would by following a plough, or making shoes, or working coal or iron. You feel that you will be worth your salt because of watching out for the interests of others.

That is your feeling. But believe me, when I assure you, that it is the common feeling of the whole human race, and has been the common feeling right from time immemorial. The world has always been full of would-be managers of the affairs of others. If you don't believe this, all I can say is that you don't realize how vast is the egotism of our common humanity. We would all like to be statesmen. Even I, myself, would think twice before I refused a job as a Cabinet Minister.

And that is the whole trouble, my good labour members. The whole lot of us would like to be grand and great, and be in receipt of five thousand of the best per year.

Seriously, there has been far too much bossing in the world. People have known too much about others and not enough about themselves. And, if you will just use your heads a bit, you will see that this instinct to boss is at the root of nearly all the load of trouble that the human race has to carry. One country knows exactly what is right and proper for another country. One race can tell another race all about it. And so we have wars, and countries armed to the teeth so as to be ready to make wars.

You will say that this is human. Of course it is. And I will also add that it was once human for the men of England to eat one another. But we managed to get over that kind of humanity.

And therefore we don't want you to be copying the rude and arrogant ways of the rulers whom you think you are going to dispossess. We don't want your asinine talk about Socialism. We Englishmen are not going to have you plunge in deeper into the mud than we are plunged already. We have our faults, but we like freedom.

I know that landlords and lords and dukes are a dreadful lot, but if you can show me that men from the working class are any better when through craft or chance they get into responsible positions then I will say no more.

So don't be rude and arrogant, you men who represent labor, for the world must advance, and changing one old man of the sea for another is a poor way of advancing.

You can only be of use to progress if you prove that you are finer and wiser and kinder than the people who grasped the reins of affairs before.

OF COURSE IT IS a grand thing to put the truehearted man who voices your ideals into Parliament, for now he will be able to do something effective in the way of running England for England's good.

If anything goes wrong, he is the man who will give 'em what for in the House of Commons! No insolent, Front Bench aristocrat will be able to keep him down! Why, to keep down your true-hearted and strong-voiced member would be like trying to keep down a volcano!

And so, after the election is over, you sit down and rest easy. And, as you rest, a glow of satisfied pride steals through you. You are glad and thankful that you have done your poor suffering country a bit of good.

You sit down and take a well-deserved rest. You are glad that you worked as you did work for the true-hearted man.

For years things have not gone well with England. The traitors who were so long in power had done their deliberate best to ruin the country! To tell the truth, their perfidy did not dawn upon you in quite the way it ought to have dawned upon you till you heard the orations of the man with the true heart whom you have now helped to put where he can really do some good. He pictured their vices for you in the strongest of strong lights. Indeed, there were moments when his scathing denouncements made you wonder how such people had managed to keep out of jail.

But even that is not the main point. The main point is that you have now put into Parliament a powerful and virile man who by the force of his personality will make himself felt as a power for good. You have got a strong man into the council chamber of the nation.

And as you sit down, taking your well-deserved rest, you dream dreams.

How this lion of debate will thunder forth if anything goes wrong. In dreams you hear the swelling tones of his resonant and reaching voice. In dreams you see his eyes flash, as his opponent wilts and withers before him. The be-wigged Speaker listens to him with awed respect. Sleepy members shake themselves from their sleepiness as he grandly denounces Wrong and sets up on its pedestal, Right. His wit pierces as a sword. By the force of himself and his eloquence he sets things going as they ought to go. He is a grand person, this true-hearted man with the resonant and ringing voice. And you dream on.

A beautiful dream, but alas, alas, only a dream.

For your true-hearted man who voices your ideals has as much power in the House of Commons as a feather has in a gale of wind. No one wilts or withers before him, the Speaker is in no way awed by him, and the tired members sleep the sleep of the just in the midst of the fire of his oratory. His wit falls flat and level even as the dull waters of the ditch. Your true-hearted member is just a common ordinary nobody who must do absolutely as he is told. And even if he should turn out to be the lion of your dream, he will have no more power in the historic House than a baby. And not only will he have no power. He will be pushed out of his seat the first chance that comes along, for there is room only in the historic House for men who will vote like machines.

He must do as he is told by the Party, or be one who is utterly and absolutely useless. He must sign himself over body and soul to the Whip. If he won't, out he goes.

Your member has less power than the ordinary voter at a General Election, for the ordinary voter can vote as his alleged intelligence directs. But your member must vote exactly as he is told. If he won't, there are ways and means of getting him out and keeping him out, it matters not what his views are. There are methods of keeping him out even against the real wish of his constituents. For the craft and scruple of the Party is as the craft and scruple of Machiavelli. It sticks at nothing.

The meaning of the word, Party? It is this: Party means a small knot of men who wield power, and whose end and aim and ambition and object is to keep wielding power. To do this, this knot of men will sacrifice anything. It is a well-known fact in human psychology that a crowd will do things that no individual ever would do. And the Party is a small crowd.

You know the saying about a corporation—that it has neither a body nor a soul. This saying fits the Party, only that there is some check upon a corporation. But on the political Party there is none. It can do exactly and absolutely what it chooses. It can ruin, or take chances upon ruining, its country so as to keep in power. And often it does this.

It matters not what the particular name is that the Party calls itself. It is always the same—a crowd of men whose first and middle and last aim is to keep in power.

To keep in power the Party would sell England—it would ruin England—it would degrade England.

Curiously enough, an important political book has just been published which proves this fact up to the hilt. I don't suppose that it was in the least sense in the writer's mind to prove this, but he proves it, nevertheless. He shows that the small, inner, governing body, Party, thinks of itself first, second, and third, and of England not at all.

Party does not really mean a whole political body such as the Tories or the Liberals. It means the small, secret, governing clique enclosed within these bodies.

And this small governing body is responsible neither to God nor to man. It possesses powers the most absolute and monstrous, and is only out for its own interest.

The argument of course in favor of the Party is that it is corrected by its counterpart—the Party of the other side when it is in power. But practice has proved that this is not the case. Practice has shown that the Party not in power thinks as little about the welfare of England as the Party in power. Its sole object is to reign itself. And it will do any mean or discreditable thing to attain this object.

4

The People Who Govern.

T HE PEOPLE WHO GOVERN see to it that they have
the first whack at the cakes and ale.

And this is true not only of autocracies and monarchies. It is
true also of republics and all other forms of democracies. The cakes
and ale! The people who govern are practically out for nothing else.
Mankind is ever pursuing liberty. And all he gets, or ever has got,
as a reward for his pursuit is a word. A word may be a potent and
wonderful thing, but it is hardly worth the creating of a revolution
for the purpose of being able to use it. The dreadful and tremendous French Revolution was a somewhat stiff price to pay for the
word "republic." I am not saying that "republic" is not a noble and
well-sounding word. It is. It is a word that falls delightfully upon the
ear. It has a fine, free ring about it. But there are moments when it
really sounds no better than the word "autocracy." To one who has to
slave from morning till night for an insufficient living, "republic" and
"autocracy" are words with much the same meaning. Still there is no
denying that the word "republic" both looks well and sounds well.

The dreadful and bloody French Revolution however, was a somewhat fancy price for France to pay for it.

The people who govern! They always were, and are, and will be the same. It matters not whether they are pompful emperors and kings or modestly attired presidents. It matters whether they are savages who dwell in deep tropic forests, or grand and noble conspirators who are bitten by the desire to impose their own grand and pure and noble rule upon a poor and oppressed people. It matters not whether they are administrators of religion who tell you vivid fairy stories about the wonderful place that you will go to after you are dead. These people are always the same. They are—even when they least believe it—but people who are out for the first whack at the cakes and ale.

When will men escape from the domination of words?

I am in no way suggesting that the people who govern are dishonest. They are honest enough, but because a man is honest it by no means follows that it is a pleasant thing for him to crack your skull, or to force you to raise your cap or bow the knee to him as he passes, or slave for him.

If men are ever to be free they must learn that 3 and 1 make 4 just as 2 and 2 make 4. They must learn that four 1's make 4. They must learn that 8 halves make 4 exactly. They must learn that the figure 4 is 4 just as much when it is plain as when it is embossed. In short, they must learn that 4 is 4, however much it may be disguised.

At first sight it would appear that this truth—that 4 is absolutely and exactly 4—was a plain thing that all men could instantly grasp. It would seem that even the rushing, intellectual giant in the street might grip it with ease. But such is not the case. The mind of man is mysterious and paradoxical. Man has a genius for missing the thing that is right under his nose. The best way for a truth to miss him is for that truth to stare straight in his face. But don't think that I am blaming the rushing, intellectual street-giant. I am not. He is a blind man who is in good company. Some of the most famous men the world has known have been as blind as he is. Great philosophers have written immortal works which proved conclusively that 4 times 1 was an altogether different thing from twice 2.

The philosopher is often an ingenious ass.

AS A MATTER OF FACT the people who govern the world are practically in touch with one another. There is a subtle Freemasonry binding them all. They are a class that is divided neither by race, religion nor country. Of course they pretend to be divided, but this pretense is only for the benefit of the people they govern. The people who govern form a great clique that is linked together by a common interest.

The world is their oyster.

Everything is run for the sole purpose of suiting them. To go against their will is the unholiest of sacrileges. To sin against the State is to commit a sin that will bring upon you, not the mythic punishment of the world to come, but the palpable and actual punishment of the world of the hard present. The people who govern are people who—to use an apt slang saying—prefer to have money down. Should you sin against them they would laugh loudly did you offer them a promissory note on the pains of Hell.

The world is their oyster.

And really, as a general rule, any fair observer must give them credit for the skillful and deft manner in which they open it. This is their supreme faculty—this opening of the oyster. And they get this faculty direct from God!

But here, perhaps, I'd better correct myself. It is only the older hands who get their faculty direct from God. The newer people at the game get their faculty from glorious ideals. They come forth to save the world—or rather the oyster—and they end by opening it.

T HE PEOPLE WHO GOVERN ARE very touchy and dignified, even with their own kind. If the other people who govern say a word that veers in the slightest degree from the pink of diplomatic politeness they take it most seriously—or to be more exact, they make the people who possess the blessing of being governed by them take it most seriously. If diplomatic nothings be not said in such and such a manner they intimate politely that they will go to war. Or rather they intimate—with extreme politeness, of course—that the people whom they govern will go to war.

Of course, they don't go to war themselves. It would be too commonplace and too vulgar a thing for them to get in the firing line themselves. They might get shot—and then how would the people whom they govern get on? What a dreadful calamity it would be if the Prime Minister of a country, or a foreign minister, or any other sort of governing official, were to be killed in a war that he had created. It would be a stupendous and a national misfortune. Such an awful thing would never do. And I must do these people the common, ordinary justice to say that they never expose the lucky country to which they belong to the chance of any such dreadful thing happening. They have the patriotic thoughtfulness to see to it that they keep well out of harm's reach.

I would like to be allowed to come in parenthetically here and say that the people who have got on in the world see with more clearness than usual the exalted virtues of the people who govern.

Making a bit causes the scales to drop from their eyes.

Usually the people who govern declare these wars in safe and comfortable chambers. They are sorry when they are declaring them, but other governing people of the other lucky country were not polite—and so there must be satisfaction. Politeness must be maintained at all hazards.

And the intellectual giant who goes along the street is very pleased indeed that the people who govern him have a proper and a Spartan regard for the niceties of diplomatic language. His country must really keep up its dignity. And he is very satisfied indeed that some-one should go off to the wars to fight for the glory and dignity of getting the exact and right kind of words used to the people who honor him by governing him. Of course the mere trifle of going to war himself over this hardly occurs to him. But he is very willing that other people should go out to maintain the nice and exact sense of dignity of the people who govern.

The contractors are also very pleased. It is most pleasant at once to make a bit and to add to the honor and glory of prime ministers and foreign ministers, and kings and emperors and presidents. To help the grand old flag to flutter in a dignified manner and to make a bit at the same time is soothing and satisfying.

And so it is that everyone is pleased. The people who govern, and the intellectual street-giant, and the contractor who makes a bit—and a good bit—in a lofty and patriotic cause.

Often as not the maker of a bit does not belong to the country off whom he is making a bit. But this matters nothing. He is after all engaged in a splendid and soothing and glorious work. He is helping along the cause of national honor.

And everyone is pleased and gratified. And tuneful and inspiring bands play off the men who go forth to do the mere bit of fighting.

THERE ARE SOME RUDE and wrong-headed thinkers who assert that the time will come when there will be no people who govern—when men will govern themselves. I, myself, at the beginning said that those who govern were only out for the first whack at the cakes and ale. But light has suddenly come to me. And I now beg to recant.

Concentration on the subject has shown me my error. And I must also ask pardon for my vulgar simile about people who govern opening the oyster. I am wrong. The oyster opens itself.

Yes, these rude and wrong-headed thinkers say that the time must come when all the people who now govern will have to go to work, it matters not whether they rule towns and cities or kingdoms and empires.

But these thinkers are surely only malicious people who have no sense of the light and honor and dignity that is shed upon all the lucky people of the world by the people who govern. And if anyone has ever thought that I was in any way related to this wrong-headed band I sincerely hope that they will see that now I am not. The light has come to me.

After all, who can blame anyone for eating a fresh beautiful oyster that opens itself?

In my humble view these alleged thinkers, who say that men would be better off if they had no one to govern them, are a danger to the community.

Man is in general as an oyster that opens itself. He will always be so despite anything that rude thinkers may say to the contrary. And even if it does come to pass as the rude thinkers say, it would be a very bad thing indeed—for how then could man enjoy the honor and glory and dignity and blessings generally that are showered so plenteously upon him by the people who govern?

5

Pawns In The Game.

FROM THE TIME OF THE CONQUEST up to now there has been struggling as to which class should have the power of absolute rule in England.

First it was the men of the kingly class who had the power of absolute rule. England was an autocracy. But along came the bold, bad barons. And lo! John was made to sign all sorts of things at Runnymede. And autocracy passed. And fair England was now ruled by the noble barons. True, the King had a say. But it was only what you might call a polite kind of a say. The barons held the ace-spots.

You must not think that the barons made John sign the Magna Carta just because of the power that lay in their own good right arms. For if you thought this, you would think wrong. The truth of the matter is that the barons had many thousands of good, simple, stout men-at-arms, who would fight to the death at a word. And this fact was plain to the kingly John when he was doing his bit of penmanship at Runnymede.

In a word, these good, simple, stout men-at-arms were pawns in the game.

History is silent as to what they got out of the game. But the fact that they remained pawns could not be covered up by a thousand silences. The barons became more gay and sporty than ever. There was now no absolute ruler to keep them in order.

But the men-at-arms, and their kind, still remained pawns.

And lo! here was the Black Death! And it came to pass that the pawns got a bit of their own back. One John Ball[20], a fine priest, had fought for them. This priest was the bravest of the brave. He fought for the welfare of the pawns in the game. And he refused to ask a pardon from the King.

And John Ball was hanged, drawn, and quartered at St. Albans on July 15, 1381. This great and heroic priest was foully murdered by the barons—men of the class who had despoiled King John so that they themselves might have absolute power.

---

20   John Ball (c. 1338 – July 15, 1381) was an English priest who took a prominent part in the Peasants› Revolt of 1381. He was born and lived in St. Albans, Hertfordshire, later moving to Norwich and then to Colchester during the plague years of the Black Death. The country was exhausted by death on a massive scale and crippling taxes; the Black Death was followed by years of war, which had to be paid for. The population was nearly halved by disease and overworked, and onerous flat-rate poll taxes were imposed.

Ball was imprisoned in Maidstone, Kent, at the time of the 1381 Revolt. What is recorded of his adult life comes from hostile sources emanating from the religious and political social order. He is said to have gained considerable fame as a roving preacher without a parish or any link to the established order and his insistence on social equality.

His utterances brought him into conflict with the Archbishop of Canterbury, and he was thrown in prison on several occasions. He also appears to have been excommunicated, owing to which, in 1366 it was forbidden for anyone to hear him preach. These measures, however, did not moderate his opinions, nor diminish his popularity. He took to speaking to parishioners in churchyards after the official services: in English, the "common tongue," not the Latin of the clergy, a radical political move. Ball was "using the bible against the church," very threatening to the status quo.

Shortly after the Peasants' Revolt began, Ball was released by the Kentish rebels from his prison. When the rebels had dispersed, Ball was taken prisoner at Coventry, given a trial in which, unlike most, he was permitted to speak. He was hanged, drawn and quartered at St. Albans in the presence of King Richard II on July 15, 1381. His head was displayed stuck on a pike on London Bridge, and the quarters of his body were displayed at four different towns.

This splendid priest died for the pawns in the game. But his name will live forever in the sacred roll of the heroes who have died for liberty.

Centuries passed and there slowly arose another power. The power of the trader, the power of the middleman, the power of wealth. This power exists at this present moment. And there are signs that it is about to be questioned. There are signs that it must make room for another power.

But what of the pawns?

Will they receive anything more from the new power than they did from the old?

The English working classes are worse off now than they have been at any time since the Conquest. They endure more starvation and misery and degradation than they have ever endured before.

What will they get from the new power? What will they get from Socialism?

Nothing. Less than nothing. Socialism will plunge them deeper into the mire of slavery. For Socialism is an extension and an intensifying of the power of the State.

Socialism is the trust system writ very large indeed. Bad though the present system is, unjust though it is, it is infinitely better than Socialism. For in the present system a man has some chance to grow.

I am of the working class, and I am sorry for the working class.

But I am afraid of these Labour leaders. I fear these men who are more arrogant and domineering than men such as the descendants of the old feudal barons.

I tell you, men of my own class, to beware of them. They are going in a wrong direction. You cannot cure slavery by enslaving the people still further. And you know, men of the working class, how arrogant and domineering some of these Labour men are when they get into a position of power. I will not name names. But you know. Don't misunderstand me. I speak at no man's bidding. I am free, and the reason I am free is because I am an individual.

I only warn you that the Labour leaders are steering you on a wrong course. The State is too strong as it is. We don't want to have it made a million-fold more strong.

In a state of Socialism you will still be pawns in the game. You will still be ground down by cunning manipulators of votes.

A time will come when you will not be pawns in the game. But it will not come by the way of the dread slavery of Socialism.

Bart Kennedy
On Art and Beauty

"John Bour"[?]. Barefooted, shabbily dressed man, sitting on crates, in front of
brick wall, with arm around a cat, holding a bottle of Raleigh Rye whiskey

1

Concerning Art And Artists.

T HE FIRST THING THAT STRUCK me about the
Academy was that it was a place where were gathered together
numerous pictures of noble, distinguished and beautiful persons. I
had no idea that millionaires and their sons and daughters were so
kind-looking and fine-looking and ideal. I made a vow never again
to write or speak disrespectfully of millionaires. For I was awed and
chastened by the splendor of their lofty brows and their look of
idealism.

I was glad that I had expended my shilling. And the thought came
to me that if President Roosevelt would come over and do likewise
he would revise his rude language concerning millionaires. He would
see that they were persons of beautiful thoughts—that the word
poetic was not too strong a word to apply to them.

And as I went on tramp through the Academy it occurred to me
that the "Royal Academy of Arts" was hardly the best name for this
splendid place. Rather should it be called the "Palace of Vindication
of the True Character of Millionaires."

What noble brows, what tender mouths, what— But I must stop. I must not allow my enthusiasm to gallop me away.

But, ere I pass on, let me pay a tribute to the keenness and penetration of eye of the artists who were allowed the privilege of painting these beings. Let me salute these Balzacs of the brush! These discoverers of deep-hidden, mystic, beautiful human qualities!

Frankly, I was disappointed with the Academy. But not in the way you would suppose. The professional art critic had led me to think that it was a place packed up with commonplace pictures. But such is not the case. I fear that the professional art critic is as other professional critics. He is an authoritative, exacting person who can do nothing, and who feels that he is dowered with a divine right to tell the earth all about something just because he knows nothing about this something.

He says the pictures in the Academy are commonplace. Or rather he says that the general trend of work in the Academy is without value.

I don't agree. I have never been in the Academy before, but I have been in art galleries in other parts of the world, and I must say that in my view the Academy holds its own with any gallery I have been in, however famous. I mean it holds its own from the standpoint of being interesting. I am a man outside of art, of course, but I am as well equipped with invincible ignorance upon the subject as the most brilliant art critic that breathes. I may therefore speak authoritatively.

I am sorry, but I have no respect for the old master, who does not interest me. I care not a fig how high his price may be at Christie's. And I don't think it is fair that the new, the living, masters should be so constantly belabored with the work of the men who are dead. The same thing happens with poor unfortunate men who write for a living. A critic once said that I was not Shelley. A fact of which I was aware before he told me of it.

I will admit that the Academy is somewhat overcrowded with portraits of vulgar-looking people, vainly endeavoring to look noble and distinguished. But outside of that there are pictures in it that are great pictures and beautiful pictures.

Art must interest and charm, or it is not art. And if modern art has more interest and charm than the art of the past, let us be honest and fair enough to say it has. This worship of the past because it is the past is servile and ignorant and snobbish. The most effective modern painting is more subtle and beautiful and commanding than the painting of the past. That is, it is to me. There are pictures in the Academy that are the most beautiful pictures I have ever seen. And I don't except even the pictures in the Prado in Madrid.

The picture that I liked best of all was "The Wandering Psyche," painted by Arthur Hacker[21]. It is a study in the nude. And words cannot describe its tenderness and beauty and purity. A girl going along. Her face is strange and sad and mystical. I see the picture before me even now. The memory of it will always be with me. A study in beautiful ivory color tones. It had upon me the thrilling effect of low, strange music. Here is a work of genius. If the Academy did no more than show this noble and beautiful picture it would well justify its existence.

Near to it was a picture called "La Penseuse," a study of an old woman, by Anna Airy[22]. A picture effective and striking.

And there was a weird picture of white hounds moving in a wood in the midst of shadows. A strange picture of imagination by Maud Earl[23].

---

21 Arthur Hacker (September 25, 1858 – November 12, 1919) was an English classicist painter. In his art he was most known for painting religious scenes and portraits, and his art was also influenced by his extensive travels in Spain and North Africa.

22 Anna Airy (June 6, 1882 – October 23, 1964) was an English oil painter, pastel artist and etcher. She was one of the first women officially commissioned as a war artist and was recognized as one of the leading women artists of her generation. During World War I, Airy was given commissions in a number of factories and painted her canvases on site in often difficult and sometimes dangerous conditions.

23 Maud Alice Earl (1864–1943) was a British-American artist, known for her

I liked the ship picture by Arthur J. Black[24], "Trimming the Side-lights." A man aboard was getting the lanterns to put out on the side of the ship, as she was moving over the waters. You could feel the motion of the ship as she was moving along in the falling lights.

May I be allowed to say a word about the work of Mr. J.S. Sargent[25]? His portraits are most real and life-like, but there is somehow in them a hard effect. It is as if the pose of the subject was too set and firm. If I may so put it, his portraits seem to say too much. The keen eye of the artist sees what it is not possible for the ordinary eye to see. His portraits made me feel as if I were looking at human beings through a microscope.

It is true that the microscope reveals what exists, but I am sure that when anything is looked at too sharply or keenly the general roundness and harmony of the effect of the whole is in part lost. I would like very much to see the originals of Mr. Sargent with his subjects standing by them. I wonder if they would reveal to the ordinary eye all that their portraits tell.

It will be said, I know, that the artist ought to paint but for his own vision. But with this I do not at all agree. When art goes before an audience it must have regard for that audience. Art for art's sake is a foolish, parrot cry. It would be right enough did the artist wish

canine paintings. Her works are much enjoyed by dog enthusiasts and also accurately record many breeds. Earl became famous during the Victorian era, a time when women were not expected to make their living at painting.

24   Arthur John Black (1855–1936) was a popular landscape and portrait artist who worked in both oils and watercolors. A number of his works can be seen in many private and public galleries.

25   John Singer Sargent (January 12, 1856 – April 14, 1925) was an American expa-triate artist, considered the "leading portrait painter of his generation" for his evocations of Edwardian-era luxury.
    He enjoyed international acclaim as a portrait painter. An early submis-sion to the Paris Salon in the 1880s, his *Portrait of Madame X*, was intended to consolidate his position as a society painter in Paris, but instead resulted in scandal. During the next year following the scandal, Sargent departed for England where he continued a successful career as a portrait artist.

that no one but himself should see his work. But such is not really the case. And were there no audience, there could be no art. I should think that Mr. Sargent painted too much for himself and too little for his public.

I fear that I must now apologize for what I said in the beginning about the critics. For I find that I have just committed the crime I accused them of myself. Good old critics! Regard what I said as if it were but a mere jest. How would we be able to get on without you? Forgive me!

ART FOR ART'S SAKE MEANS that you care not for the opinion of the unfortunate people who buy your wares. It means that you care only for your own opinion. You make things for sale, and you have an utter contempt for any judgment or point of view save your own. I don't claim to be a Philistine, but really I am astonished at the cold impudence of such an attitude. I make a picture, or a piece of statuary, and I scowl at the person who is buying it if he dares even to breathe a word of criticism concerning it. Or I write an imperishable prose essay and when the poor, unfortunate, careworn editor fails to see it in the fullness of its beauty I abuse him, or I give him the eye of scorn. And should a reader have the assurance to say a word against it, I, of course, dance on him altogether.

Gentlemen! Or rather I ought to say, fellow artists! For I claim to be a sort of a rough-and-ready, come-day go-day, pot-boiling kind of an artist myself. Listen. This kind of talk won't go. I like you! You are the salt of the planetary system! This kind of thing won't wash.

I fully realize that we, artists, are the noblest people that ever happened. Did we not paint our little-nooks-in-Brittany pictures, or sculpt our sculptures, or do our impressionistic imperishable prose bits, the grass would at once stop growing! England would topple. But, even so. There is such a thing as straining the rope a bit too hard. There is such a thing as overdoing it. And I think we certainly overdo it when we give it forth to an apologetic world that we don't care a rap for the people we work for.

I once had the honor of meeting an artist who said that all that he wanted was to be let alone. I went into a certain restaurant with some friends and I was introduced to the great man. He looked at my hair, and seeing that it was closely cropped, he actually came to the conclusion that I was an outsider. And he treated me to a dose of lofty, artistic, cold scorn. But I put up with his attitude for a while, for I was curious to get at his attitude concerning things and life.

It was certainly the oddest I ever heard of. He was a very clever artist, who sold whatever he painted, but he looked upon the buyers of his works and all other people outside art—myself included—as inferior dullards and Philistines.

I listened, and then I began on him. He could paint, but he was not much of a man in the arena where ready and vivid and colorful speech-expression counts.

To do him justice he tried to hold his corner. But— Well, they led him away.

It is a sacrilegious thing to say, I know, and I say it with trembling, but I very much fear that the phrase, "Art for art's sake," is often used to excuse a lot of bad, unclear art work. If I see a picture of which I can make neither head nor tail, if I hear music that racks me, if I read a piece of prose that I cannot understand, I am told that the persons who are guilty of these weird performances are artists who care for no one's opinion but their own. They are workers at art for art's sake!

This is very well, but why then don't they keep their art to themselves? Why don't they bury it, or lock it up?

The truth is that art that can't make itself understood is no art. It you are talking to a man, and the man can't understand you, you are talking in vain.

Art is an appeal to people. If the appeal fails, it is not art.

The world's greatest artists always had the power to make themselves understood. The meaning of the work of the great Velasquez can be grasped by anyone. It shines out, clear as crystal. It would impress and hold the most dull and stupid. It is the magic of reality. It comes straight to you. After all, what is art? You don't really know, and I don't really know, and no one else really knows.

A great deal of good, useful paper has been spoiled in the endeavor to define it. But the truth of the matter is that nothing has been said further than that art is something that no one can define. I fear that the critic is a person of deep, sardonic humor.

Art for art's sake means working for something that no one knows anything about.

It is one of the phrases that has gulled an innocent world too long. As I have often pointed out, there are many such phrases lying round loose to the hurt of those who pay attention to them.

Art for art's sake!

Let us remove the fangs of this mischievous phrase. Let us pay no attention to it. Let it be dead!

It has killed many a young artist. For art-work, of whatever kind, is a trade to be learned, just as one has to learn to make shoes, or to drive a cab. Being clear in your branch of artwork is analogous to making the shoe fit rightly and steering the cab safely.

You may not believe it, my youthful artistic friend, but stating a thing clearly in art-work is not as easy as it looks. The funny idea you have in your head won't make the people smile or laugh unless you write it just so. The profound, deep, wise, poetic thought won't thrill the native unless you put it so that his intellect will grip it at once. You must always be clear. Your music, picture, or statue must appeal with its effect instantly. It doesn't matter what you intend your effect to be, whether comedy, tragedy, mystery, or beauty. Always be clear.

And people will buy your wares.

You will perhaps tell me that some artists have never bothered about being clear and still have got on. But they are very rare exceptions. Their work is not good work. In fact, it would get no hearing at all but for a few moony faddists. Never mind the faddists. It is the good old general easy ordinary public you must mind. The butcher and the draper and the baker know a bit more than you think they know. They don't know the tricks of your trade, but they know when they like your work. And that is enough for you.

I know where the art for art's sake touch comes in. It comes in when you've got an idea you can't make clear. And you get vexed when the people don't understand you, and pass on.

Don't do it, my boy. Learn to be direct in your efforts. And then they won't pass on.

And pay no attention to the person who tells you that art is too noble and beautiful and ideal a pursuit to be profaned by thoughts of making a living out of it. Remember that the best work has, in nine hundred and ninety-nine cases out of a thousand, been done by professional men who had to live by the exercise of their craft.

To learn deftness and accuracy in art-work needs a great amount of practice and care and concentration, it matters not what your attitude for the work may be. And you ought to be paid for your time and attention. And if you feel it to be a disgrace to get money for your work, remember that greater artists than you can ever hope to be did not think it to be a disgrace.

And don't despise your audience—your public. It is snobbish and unfair and silly. You are in the position of doing work that you hope people will look at and buy, and at the same time making a pretense that you care nothing for their judgment. Such an attitude of mind is ridiculous and undignified.

Work for the public. Always have them in your mind. And remember that they don't especially commission you to do works of genius. They don't force you to go and starve in a garret. They don't tell you to go off and starve in the Latin Quarter. Neither do they tell you to go and write mighty world-shaking books. In fact, the poor, unfortunate public has so much to do looking out for itself that it hasn't time to bother with you.

So don't be severe. But aim to do your work so that your intended meaning will be clear. And pay no attention to that absurd and foolish phrase:

Art for art's sake!

A WORD OR TWO MORE:
It is all very well for artists to talk about the immense amount of good they do in the world, but the truth of the matter is that they are just as averse to the doing of the world's real work as the Cabinet Minister, or the capitalist, or the Bishop, or the Judge, or the interesting footpad who borrows money from the passer-by without even being formally introduced.

I like artists, for, taking them by and large, they are the nicest of fellows. But I wish they had more sense of humor. I wish they could see that the grass would still grow even if they stopped producing masterpieces.

Why, my dear artists, the world would still go on if I, even I, were to stop indulging in my imperishable prose.

I will pass on to the further consideration of the relation that the work of the artist bears to the real work of the world.

In the first place, let me ask you, my dear artist, if you have ever carried the hod? I am not talking now to the artist who is just beginning. I am talking to the artist who makes his thousands a year by the immortalizing of the lofty and dignified features of millionaires.

Have you ever, my dear artist, carried the hod? I know that you have gone hungry. I know—but we will not go into painful details. Have you ever carried the hod?

Well, if you haven't, I have. And believe me when I assure you that carrying the hod, my good fellow-artist, is what you might call work. I say fellow-artist advisedly, for I, like you, manage to exist without the doing of real work. And men who can do this are obviously artists.

Listen, artists. Nobody wants to do the real work of the world. Let us away with bunkum. We all want to be well paid for being great and grand and distinguished.

And there is the top and bottom and the front and the back of the whole business. You can all talk till you are blue in the face, and when you are finished that is all there is in it. The artist is a shirker from the world of real labor.

And I am not saying that I mind this. I am a shirker myself. But what I do mind is the lack of humor that does not allow an artist to see this truth.

I have a friend who works at my own trade of writing. He is a very well known man, and he once spoke to me of the absolute and vital importance of writing to the community at large. According to him things would be in a bad way if books were not written. I fear that I replied to him in a jocose and playful spirit.

The truth of the matter is that art—root and stem and branch—is the appanage[26] of the ruling power. And even when art is revolutionary, it is impelled, consciously or unconsciously, by the instinct to be itself the ruling power.

But apart from all this there is the question of the relation between art and labor. This relation may be likened to a man who is mounted on a horse. Labor carries art even as the horse carries the man.

---

26 "Appanage" from 17th-century Old French: to provide land and or money in support of a family member.

Let it not be thought that I mean to suggest that the people who labor are fine people. They are not. They have been slaves too long to be fine people. But the fact of the matter is that it is they alone who do the world's real work. In practice, the artist is of the class who lives off them. Just as I am.

The time, of course, will come when art will not be the specialized thing that it is now. But that time is as yet very far distant. The time will come when labor will not be the thing of shame that it is at present. The time will come when all people will do labor with the hands. It is not a good thing that a man should be working at art through the whole of the time. It is not a good thing that he should be forever writing books, or painting pictures, or making statuary. In one way it is as bad for a man to be always working at art as it is for him to be always doing rude and violent labor.

Still, this is not the point that I wish especially to bring out. The point I wish to bring out is that the artist is utterly and absolutely dependent upon the laborer for his existence. For this the artist practically gives the laborer no return.

The paymaster of the artist is the person who sweats the laborer. And there you are. The laborer pays the piper, and he hears nothing of the tune. He is too far away from the whole business.

Museums? You tell me that he can go and see immortal works in museums? Why, my good artist, the laborer is too tired to be bothered about going to museums. He would sooner have his pipe and his glass of beer. And he is a good judge. However, I don't want to get too serious. But I do want the artist to have enough sense of humor to realize he is of the class who do none of the world's real work. I want him to realize that he is lucky not to be carrying the hod—or sitting in an office adding up two and two.

And I would also like to hear less about his mission. But here I must in justice say that the real top-notch artist is as quiet as a mouse concerning his mission. He is satisfied to do his work, and after that to relieve the good old tradesperson of as much as possible of the cash that the tradesperson has stolen from the laborer.

It is a merry and a comic world, my good artist lads. A world where it doesn't do to get too much vexed. Especially when one has so soft and easy a time as we artists have.

2

World-Town Pictures.

I T IS PERHAPS A STRANGE THING to say, but the first thing that impresses me about London is its quietude. I expect to be confounded by appalling noise. But it is not so. The stupendous town gives out almost an effect of silence.

There is confusion. The movements of the passing myriads are involuted in an extraordinary way. A sense comes upon you that these people are going nowhere. And coming from nowhere. They give out the idea that they are moving and passing in and out and going and coming aimlessly. Moving myriads inextricably mixed up and confused.

Whenever I am in London the wonder comes to me that there are so many people who are doing nothing. It is as if all men had left their avocations. As if the whole world had elected to come to this stupendous town but to pass and repass. I begin to wonder who it is that does the world's work. Surely not these aimlessly moving myriads. One knows that people are off through the land working from day into dark in workshops. That there are towns where blackened and grime-faced men toil and delve. That people work in fields.

But when this comes to the mind it is thrust forth again by these immense, passing crowds of London. Here are millions. Millions who do no work, but pass along day by day. I am appalled at the vastness of the throngs. Always going. It is as if the whole world had concentered here to move in a confused, inconceivably vast horde.

I said that the thing that most impresses me about London is its quietude. It is quiet when compared with other great capitals. But in time the sense of its quietude leaves you. You feel the dominance and the magnetism of great sound. It has passed into you. You are of it. It had seized you from the outset, but it is only now that you sense its effect.

London is a town of sound. And for me there is a wondrous music in this sound. For me it is a magical, illimitable, indescribable voice. A voice that it is not given to me to understand. But a voice that appeals to me. That seizes me.

Other great capitals are places of huge disquieting noise. But London is a labyrinth where sound reigns immense and glorious and consonant. When first you are confronted with London it may well be that you are appalled. This amazing titanic town overwhelms you. Your mind blenches. You do not understand. You are in a place of myriads where reign movement and sound.

But the time will perhaps come to you when you will love this gigantic town. When you will love to wander through it. And when this time comes there will be for you no other town in the world. The passion will have seized you. You will care not for the great towns of the world that are brilliant and gay and bright.

This will come to pass should you feel the thrall of this gigantic and mysterious London. You will read meanings into the sounds of London, its bells. As you pass along, thoughts inscrutable and vague will come to you. The voice of London will speak to you and reveal secrets that you may not tell. You will go along, thrilled by its life.

Think not that London is but a vast place of great, grey undertones. Think not this, for there are times when London glows with
a magical and transcendent beauty.

There are days when London is clear-aired and filled with a golden
shining. Joyful days—full of a soft, strange glow. Golden, strange days
of light when the immense sounding labyrinth is illumed and transfigured. Dream days. Days when the sounds of the bells of London
come to you as golden, wondrous voices. Happy, joyful, clear days.

It is beautiful then to go along through the passing myriads. For
then you are living within the romance and charm of London. You
are bathed in the glow of a city vast and mysterious and magical.
You are in a place of enchantment illimitable.

But I love the great, grey undertones.

As I walk I ponder upon their meanings. For could I but read
them it might be that to me was revealed the mystery of life and
humanity. What might I not know, could I but read the meanings
of London's great, grey undertones?

These undertones are as voices telling of obscure myriads who
live down in London's depths.

I hear them as I pass along. Even when the bells come as golden,
wondrous voices, I hear these great, grey undertones. Ever are they
living beneath the sound that reigns over London.

Why they should appeal to me I know not. Why they should
always be with me as I pass along I cannot tell. Often I wonder if
others hear them. Do they speak to the myriads that pass and pass?

Mysterious undertones, weird and strange, and vague and inscrutable. Like unto voices from out depths. What is it that you are telling?

Great, grey undertones of London! What do you presage?

The moods of London!

Always they are changing. Passing one into the other. Passing
even as pass the crowds.

Moods, grim and sad and tragical and terrible. Sinister, menacing
moods that are on the mighty town in days of strange darkness. These

moods grim and menacing! I fear them not as I pass undertones, along. To me they are akin to the great, grey overtones.

Talk not to me of great, set pageants and great, set shows! For there is no pageant such as the pageant that goes and goes hour by hour and day by day through the stupendous London. For me there is no place such as this town of immenseness inconceivable. Where reigns immense and glorious and mysterious sound, where live great, grey undertones, where people pass and pass and come and go—as if coming from nowhere and going nowhere, where live mysteries, brooding, immense, and strange, where glow days of magical and transcendent beauty—clear-aired, joyful days filled with golden shining. Where reigns Egyptian darkness, where live moods mysterious and great, menacing and sinister.

Talk not to me of set pageants and great, set shows! For here in this London is a pageant illimitably mightier than any pageant the world has known. This great, grey vast immenseness that holds within itself the world, and the meaning of the world, life, and the meaning of life, death, and the meaning of death, joy, tragedy, sorrow, light, darkness! Come, thou, and behold! Nor flinch, nor stand apart! But mingle, thou, into the midst of these moving myriads!

G O ALONG THE STRAND and you are in touch with the world in passing.

For this is the place to which men come who make long, far journeys. If you are thinking of a man whom years ago you saw in a far-off, foreign place, it may be well that you will see his face in this magical street. This Strand is the meeting-place of world-wanderers. They come, and they are gone, and they come again.

There is an ease of movement about the people who pass along the Strand. And they wear a leisured air. As if time were to them a thing of no especial moment. They rush not along as do the hard-faced men in the City. There is neither bustle nor eagerness nor excitement.

The human current flows evenly and steadily. In its movement there is a sense of strange rhythm. It is as if the world were passing gently before you. The wonder of the myriad-peopled world is revealing itself.

Rank, fashion, race, poverty, circumstance! Rich and poor, old and young, merry and gay, sad and sorrowful. Erect people of the open air, pale people of the narrowness of slums, dark-hued foreign people, yellow people of the mysterious East, black people from out far lands of fire. People of vice and crime, people with fine faces, with noble faces, people with mean and terrible and sinister faces, bold-faced confident people of travel and adventure, stay-at-home people, jaunty men with the fine swagger born of the bearing of arms, men with shadows in their faces, men with fear in their faces, rich and poor, old and young, merry and gay.

All passing.

All slowly passing in the mid of the sounds of the town.

A slow passing, magical picture in the midst of sound. A world moving in epitome. The races of men passing in the bonds of brotherhood. Rank, fashion, race, and poverty bound in a truce. All going together. Passing and repassing, crossing and recrossing, weaving and interweaving.

Going with a rhythm in the midst of sound.

This is the world-street of the mightiest world-town that man has known. It is no street of pomp and show and outside magnificence. Just a common thoroughfare through which humanity passes.

Day in, day out, year in, year out, the people are going along. An inexhaustible tide of beings, carrying their histories in their faces.

How wonderful is the Strand when it is filled with the soft, burning gold of the sun! How strange then are the passing faces!

How weird is the Strand when upon it has fallen the gloom and dimness of a winter day! When upon it has fallen the fog of London. The people pass then as shadows through a great shadow. The Strand is then a great, grey shadow. A still, vast shadow through which shadows are weaving and interweaving. The people are as amorphous ghosts. And lights dimly burn. And voices arise. You are here in the midst of the passing of ghosts. In the midst of a confusion.

Around you are strange muffled sounds. And suddenly a white face is close to you. And it is gone. And the fog deepens. And lo! There is stillness in the Strand.

Give me the Strand in the mid of day when the sun shines clear. I love to go along it then through the moving throngs and look towards the old, strange river as I pass. For the sun shines on the river, and the reflection shines up again in the strangely-shaping clouds. Moving throngs and shining, strangely-shaping clouds. As I go along they seem somehow to be at one in my mind. And there comes to me a curious fancy. It is that these men-throngs are but as the cloud-throngs that appear and dissolve. Coming from nowhere. Going nowhere. Just passing. A curious, strange, weird phantasmagoria, coming, passing, shaping and re-shaping here under the clear light of the sun. What means this flowing multitude of humans? Here today gone tomorrow. In life, out of life. But as clouds. Meaning no more. Meaning no less. What are these hopes, and ambitions, and fears, and thoughts of the morrow, and thoughts of the past that surround me?

Only clouds.

These passing humans mean no more. They move in the midst of the thing called time but as the clouds move. These men are but things of dream and phantasy. Dreams and phantasies passing in and out of the wondrous mystery, Life.

I am passing in the clear light in the midst of dreams!

Again, there are times when I feel that all these people that are passing are, each of them, the result and the last word of all the powers that lie in the world and the heavens. I feel that man is greater than all. I am astounded at the mystery of the power that lives within him. This being at once so small and mighty. This lord of incalculable power who holds in his grip the world. How wondrous the arising of this being of a power inconceivable!

This being, dominant and splendid and terrible.

And as I go along through the sounds and the throngs it comes to me that man is the very apex of the life of the world. Out of the void came the world, and lo! man appeared! And man will pass, and the world will go back to the void.

And I feel that these splendid and magical beings will live again and again in other worlds. They are passing on a profound and stupendous journey, even as they are passing here before my eyes.

This Strand is the world moving in epitome.

Going day in and day out, year in and year out, marking the hour of life.

A passing, stupendous, wonderful show.

Going and coming, coming and going. A slow passing, magical, rhythmical picture.

Moving in sound.

YOU WATCH THEM—and they give out a sense of barely perceptible movement as do live people when they are grouped in stage pictures. You pass along through the great room, and there—in front of you—is a figure in modern dress. It stands by a group of figures that tells of a time gone hundreds of years. Here is the present and the past. But lo! to your amazement the modern figure moves and walks off. So subtle is the wizardry of the art in this great room that you mistake living and breathing figures for waxen figures that are moveless and still.

This exhibition of Madame Tussaud's is the epitome of the life of the world. It presents without comment life's myriad-sidedness. Here you will see the presentiment of beings who are called magnificent and squalid and criminal and glorious. And you will be taught that great foundational truth—that men are in the essence much alike. You will be taught that there is often not a pin to choose between the murderer who was interred in lime and the successful soldier who was interred in Westminster Abbey. You will see men with fine faces whose memory lives but in the annals of infamy. You will see men with crafty, terrible, sinister faces, whose deeds and lives are emblazoned and enshrined in the glorious pantheon. You will be taught that Chance is a genie of a power unimaginably greater than resolution or force of will, or even circumstance.

A strange place, this Madame Tussaud's.

Read not the partisan books that men call histories. Pore not over tomes that are alleged to reconstruct the past. For there is no magic in them save an occasional magic of style.

For me this great room of the moveless, waxen figures is a weird and wonderful place. Its wizardry conjures up the past and the present. It is as if I were looking into a magical picture. As if time itself were an immense revolving thing that had stopped suddenly and was showing in a petrified clearness things living and things dead. A magical, silent room.

Of ghosts and phantoms.

And still a place of the real. Of men, of things, of times.

The fourth George!

I like the face of this English king. Surely was he a fine, gay, devil-may-care artist of a man. This dashing, elegant fellow who was dubbed the first gentleman of Europe! History says many things about him, but who is to go by that? History is merely the safe libeling of an epoch or of a man. Here before you is the face of the man who sat on England's throne. It is a generous, vital, intelligent face. The face of one who was wise enough to know the joy of life. I care not for kings, but it is not for me to say that there have not been kings who were fine men. And if I must be ruled, rather let me be ruled by a king than by a tradesperson who becomes a president. A king is a man before he is a king, and this fourth George was a man and a fine man. Gay? Of course he was gay and dashing and a lover of art and of women. And why not? If kings there must be, at least let them be neither sour nor meddling. Let them be gay and jovial and easy. As this George.

The third George!

Let us pass him by. He has not the face of one who might worthily fill a high place.

Let us take the figures in this great room haphazard, neither following rule nor plan.

Here is Bismarck!

His face is great and hard and round. The face of a tiger. We need fighting men in the world. But we don't need butchers. This Bismarck was only a great, slaying human butcher. One who crushed liberty so that he might build up the big slave-state called Germany. Look at his face. It speaks for itself. This big Prussian Hun.

How fitly and well would he adorn the chamber of horrors.

The men we want in the world are men such as this fine Garibaldi who is here before you. He was a patriot in the truest and best sense. The Prussian butcher, Bismarck, was not fit to tie the strings of the shoes of this hero. This man fought not only for Italy. He fought for liberty—for the oppressed of the whole world. We all owe this great and splendid Garibaldi a debt. He is the finest of all the soldiers in this great, strange room.

He is finer than any king or emperor or prince that you see around you. Bow in reverence to his memory as you pass.

How grand is the face of Verdi, the great musician of Italy who wrote immortal operas. Say not that his beautiful, human, soul-stirring music will fade into a half-forgetfulness. Say not that it is the music of the past. Say not that it will not live. For it will live as long as lives human emotion and passion.

This fine Verdi! He wove for humanity sound-pictures glorious and magical.

The kings of the past!

They are ranged here before you. Here is Richard Coeur-de-Lion. Did this king of old look as looks his presentment here in this room? Has the artist caught the form and the spirit of this warrior? It surely must be so, for here before you is the presentment of a man, fine and hard and indomitable. This Richard lived in the days when kings were kings because they were kings. The artist has given a figure that fits perfectly the traditions that have been handed down to us.

And John from whom the old barons forced the signing of the Magna Charta. He is here in the act of being forced to lay the bulwark of English liberty. And Isabella with the handsome and sinister face. And Chaucer, the great man of English letters. These three significant figures are here together.

This strange room tells England's story as no book can tell it. It tells of her struggles, her achievements, her magnificence, her victories. You read this story in the faces that are moveless and still. Here are the fighting sailors and the soldiers—here are the kings and the men who grasped the helm of State. And the thinkers and the orators and the men of science and letters and art. And the adventurous men of England who travelled out into the unknown.

Nay, this room tells a larger story than even the story of England. It tells the world's story. Here are grouped the world's significant figures. Some of them benign, some of them sinister.

These figures stand here through the days and through the years. Moveless and still. And the people who are living come in and pass and repass and go back again into the move and the roar of London. They come from out the immense sounding life of the world-town into this great room of silence where it is as if Time were an immense revolving thing that had stopped suddenly.

Ever they pass through this moveless world.

You go clanking down the stone steps and you find yourself in the Chamber of Horrors.

A moment before you were up on the floor above with kings and queens and princes and the other notabilities of the world. And it may well have been that you felt a reluctance to the coming down into this chamber where are presented the figures of those who live in the annals of infamy. You felt, perhaps, that it would be a trial to your nerves.

But to your astonishment you experience no sensation of horror. For the faces here are but as the faces of those you pass in ordinary life.

Or, perhaps, I might say this: If there be any real difference between these faces and the ordinary living faces of those you pass in the streets, it is that they are stronger. And that is all. These people of the found-out crimes obviously possessed will power.

Almost all these moveless faces show intelligence, and some of them show intellect. Indeed, many of these criminals possessed fine heads—heads with broad, high frontal developments and firm chins. Charles Peace[27] was undoubtedly a man of intellect. Fowler[28] was a fine specimen of the fighting type of man. It is only fair to

---

27   Charles Frederick Peace (May 14, 1832 – February 25, 1879) was an English burglar and murderer, who embarked on a life of crime after being maimed in an industrial accident as a fourteen-year-old boy.

         After killing a policeman in Manchester, he fled to his native Sheffield, where he became obsessed with his neighbor's wife, eventually shooting her husband dead. Settling in London, he carried out multiple burglaries before being caught and wounding the policeman who arrested him. He was linked to the Sheffield murder, and tried at Leeds Assizes. Found guilty, he was hanged at Armley Prison. His story has inspired many authors and film producers.

28   Henry Fowler (b. ? – June 9, 1896) was a strongman in a traveling carnival and part-time thief. He and partner Albert Milsome robbed and killed wealthy miser Henry Smith. The case was a notorious example of the "cut-throat" defense, where the criminals blame each other for the crime. In this case, both were found guilty and hanged.

say, however, that the murder he committed was not a murder of premeditation.

You will be struck by the lack of the signs of degeneracy amongst these people. At the most there are but three or four degenerates amongst them, notably Burke and Hare.

Lombroso! His writings concerning crimes and criminals are fustian and nonsense. If you think of him at all, you will see how utterly the faces in this chamber confute his labored reasoning. But he is a man of science. And the chief end and aim of men of science is to show the world that they are absolutely and incontrovertibly right. Even though they may not know it this is their aim. Men of science are notorious for the discovery of dead, blank walls.

The mystery of human nature is too immense and subtle for Lombroso or any other man to penetrate. Crime is in the main but a word used to stigmatize the deeds of found-out criminals. And the real truth of the matter is that the memory of the greatest enemies of the human race is enshrined not in the annals of infamy, but in gold and state and imperishable marble.

And here a word of praise will not be out of place for this fine artist, John Tussaud, uses no artifice to make the criminals look horrible. He just gives them as they looked in life. I have often noticed that when a man is tried and found guilty of murder the person who draws the picture of the condemned for the press invariably manages to give the condemned a sinister expression. Tussaud is above this. With the instinct of the born artist he realizes the utter foolishness of those who endeavor to define and to dogmatize. He gives things to the life.

If you wish to see really venomous faces you must not look for them especially among criminals. Rather must you look for them amongst those who sit in judgment upon their fellows. Go to murder trials and study the faces of the judges and the faces of those who are being tried for their lives. Then you will see what I mean. As a class judges have the most villainous and sinister faces of any human beings. Rarely is there anything noble in the face of a judge. Anyone with eyes to see will bear me out in this. The reason of this is because life is a dreadful and a murderous thing, and these successful lawyers are the paid agents of those who are on top—those who "legally" murder and rob and crush the mass of human beings. If you wish to study sinister and mean and cruel faces, study the faces of judges.

Come not to the Chamber of Horrors.

Not that there are not some cold and dreadful faces in this chamber. There are. Take the face of Neill Cream[29] and the faces of the two women poisoners of Liverpool[30].

The face of Neill Cream is at once sinister and wheedling and destructive. But it is most certainly not the face of a degenerate. It is a powerful, able and dominant face. The forehead shows boldness and capacity, and the jaw is strong. But hard and dreadful lines are about the mouth. It is the face of a quick, daring and resolute man. And a secretive man.

---

29   Dr. Thomas Neill Cream (May 27, 1850 – November 15, 1892), was a Scottish-Canadian serial killer, who claimed his first victims in the United States and the rest in Great Britain (with the possibility of others in Canada). Cream, who poisoned his victims, was executed after his attempts to frame others for his crimes brought him to the attention of London police.

   Unsubstantiated rumors claimed his last words as he was being hanged were a confession that he was Jack the Ripper—even though he is known to have been in prison in Illinois at the time of the Ripper murders.

30   The Black Widows of Liverpool, Catherine Flannagan (b. 1829 – March 3, 1884) and Margaret Higgins (b. 1843 – March 3, 1884), were Irish sisters convicted of poisoning and murdering one person in Liverpool, England and suspected of more. The women collected a burial society payout, a type of life insurance, on each death, and it was eventually found that they had been committing murders using arsenic. Though Catherine Flannagan evaded police for a time, both sisters were eventually caught and convicted of one of the murders and both hanged on the same day at Kirkdale Prison. Modern investigation of the crime has raised the possibility that Flannagan and Higgins were known or believed by investigators to be only part of a larger conspiracy of murder-for-profit—a network of "black widows"—but no convictions were ever obtained for any of the alleged conspiracy members other than the two sisters.

Secretive power sometimes goes with quickness and force and resolution. It must not be forgotten that the mysterious thing called character is most complex and contradictory. Man is the result of dark, obscure buildings-up that have been going on and on through hundreds of thousands of years. The human brain is a terrible thing of suggestion and impulse and instinct that no one may follow. This thing that is called Consciousness knows not a tithe of what is in the brain. How idle is it therefore for the egotistic fumblers of science to make their petty definitions?

This Neill Cream was that most terrible slayer of all—the poisoner.

But let this be said. All human beings have secret and obscure and sinister promptings that they would confess to no one—perhaps not even to themselves. The one who denies this is either a fool or a liar. And that is where the value of this chamber comes to the student of men. The difference being that the criminal is the one who translates some impulse into action—or who wagnuck[31] was the realizing of some black brooding idea.

Of all the weapons of warfare the bayonet is the most sinister and evil. It is here in the Tower amongst the axes and swords and pikes and lances of the past.

A gleaming, dreadful, relentless weapon that shows a strange beauty of line as you stand and look at it from a distance. But the beauty of line is as the repelling deadly beauty shown in the lithe body of the snake. In the museums of the future men will point to this potent, horrible, devil's weapon to illustrate the lust for murder that lived in the hearts of their savage ancestors.

To me there is something fair and open in the deadliness of the sword. But the bayonet is a minister of death, mean and cruel and horrible.

---

31 "Wagnuk of a thousand claws" was a weapon used in the Maratha region of west-central India. It is worn on the hand and is said to replicate the claws of a tiger. First noted by English colonizers during the Sepoy Rebellion of 1857 and came into usage as a phrase to describe the moment of murderous clarity.

And the bayonet is modern.

It is a thing springing from out the light and knowledge of this ineffably beautiful civilization. This thrusting, twisting, infernal weapon is the pioneer of commerce. The foundation and the keeper of the greatness of nations. When the people cry out for bread it is used to bring to them content. It is used to quiet the people when they writhe under the infamous usage of the governing cliques of the world. The bayonet is the thin end of the wedge of modern civilization. And you will see it here in the Tower of London.

It gleams amongst the more decent weapons of the times of old. The fruit of a horrible, devil's idea.

This bayonet! Look well upon it! For in it you behold the potency and righteousness and light and power and sacredness and dominance of the modern State!

Old fortress of London. Wondrous old tower that has lived through a thousand years. What have you to tell us? What significance do you hold for us, the men of modern times?

Old fortress, with your weapons of death, your tremendous walls, your pomp of shining jewels, your dungeons where humans were tortured horribly, your places of devotion, your places of darkness where men slowly died in despair!

What have you to tell to us who care only for the emancipation and the liberty of human beings? What have you to tell the ones who care but little for old monstrous monuments that tell but of the crushing of our kind.

Place of strength and darkness, venerable and impressive!

Do not the ghosts of the sad and the wronged haunt you? Do not the ghosts of the murdered move within your walls through the silences of the night?

T HE STATUES LAY IN SLEEP in the hushed dimness of the abbey that stood here as on guard in the Town, heeding not the fret and change of the centuries, nor the roar nor the whirl of the surrounding immenseness, nor the hurry nor the strife of the modern phase.

This wondrous place holding within it the quietude of a strange invincibility. Arch, pillar, roof, nave and transept were held in a silence. A ghost silence.

This old Westminster Abbey. The monument to the triumphs and the glories of a mighty nation. In it slept the great men of England. Surrounding it was the roar of the mighty London.

But it waited in stillness through Time.

What tales might it not tell of magnificence of pageant, of glory of crowning of king, of solemn mien of monk and abbot, of beauty of dame, of gallant attired in his bravery, of bearing of stern warrior, of masses for the repose of souls? What might it not tell of the generations that had come and passed and gone?

This old place of dimness and shades. Wherein lay the singers of immortal songs, the strikers of mighty blows, the men of power and strength, the iron administrators, the silken courtiers—those that had travelled to lands afar and brought back treasure and advice for conquest, subtle statesmen, holders aloft of the wand of science, kings and queens and grand dames.

This stately, peaceful place. This abbey of the shades of the past. Lying holy and silent in surrounding tumult.

It brought to the mind strange thoughts as one stood within it, listening to the deep, solemn organ tone that broke and filled the silence. The sound was as a voice coming from the long dead ages.

As if the soul of the past were speaking. How small now was the vast roaring whirl of the immense, far-stretching, surrounding London!

Here were ghosts. And visions. And there came clear, magical scenes. Splendid, magical pageants of old London, and tumults and fights and the shock of arms. Shouting masses of men rushed and met. There was the redness and the flowing of blood. These pictures were as if limned in the rolling, solemn organ tone. Pictures living in wondrous sound.

And soft clear voices were sounding as angel voices heard in a dream.

And before the vision there passed a stupendous, illimitable multitude. Here were those that had lived in our England through a thousand years. A stupendous, illimitable procession. With solemn pomp kings marched with their multitudes. The darkness of the past was lifted through a thousand years.

Here in this old abbey.

A voice spoke forth the words of the Gospel. There was being told the Story that had been told through a thousand years in this abbey.

And there came silence.

Voices rose in the midst of the organ tones, chanting the praises of the mighty and glorious God. Lights burned softly in the choir. And up and afar off the red light of the dying day burned in a beautiful, strange-shaped window. This window shone softly as would shine a great jewel from out a far dimness.

Voices, soft lights, and the red light of the dying day.

A scene of magic ethereal and holy, through which passed the splendid ghost pageants of the London that was gone.

And there was opened a great door.

And through it there came a vast, harsh sound. A sound coming from a tumult immense and terrible.

The voice of the London that was living! And gone were the ghost pageants.

Here was the abbey in the mid of day. Yonder a great window was glorious with the shine of the sun. A window strangely stained and telling by rich many-colored gleamings of Christ and of His life. In fashion clear and beautiful the art of man had set forth the wondrous Tale.

The light of the mid of day lived in the window as a glorious song. A song that spoke to the soul through a profound reach of time. It was a song that the world had not yet heard, but still it lived—even though it was as if veiled with silence. It was a song that man would hear when the time came.

A song living in the midst of a silence and darkness profound.

This glorious window prefigured the light and harmony that was coming into the world.

This glorious light here in the hushed dimness of the abbey. It was the soul of this holy and reverend place. It moved slowly and strangely through the silence, falling on altar and column, moving through arch and dim transept, falling on tomb and statue, gleaming and burning gold, moving from window to window.

This soul of the old abbey. It moved strangely in the silence and the shadows. A volume as of supernal sound clothed in a garb of silence. It shone, it illumed, it transfigured this holy place.

It moved here in the mid of day.

This radiant, stupendous, surpassing spirit lived in this profound and beautiful sanctuary that man had raised to God.

And there lived again in the abbey the solemn organ tone. And again there arose the clear voices as of angels heard in a dream. And the sound of the organ and the clear voices echoed and echoed, rising higher and higher, becoming softer and softer and fainter and fainter, till they were dissolved and lost in the light that still moved and lived in the glorious windows.

The people bowed their heads in reverence. They were here in peace—away from the surrounding tumult.

The Stone of Scone.

The legend of old had it that when he whose right it was to be crowned king sat upon it groaned aloud. Thus it was that the multitude knew that they were looking upon their rightful king.

Empires had come and gone, but this stone remained. It held prisoned within it the secret of the destiny of kings. A great, dull stone.

Through thousands of years it had decreed who was the one who was to grasp the sceptre of domination. The stone of fate.

From it ran the weird, inscrutable threads of destiny. It had come from out the Afar, dim, profound.

A sandstone mass coming from the shadows.

It had held prisoned within it the secret of destiny even before this sanctuary wherein it now rested had been dreamed of by man. This Stone of Scone lying here in Westminster Abbey! It had lain through the coming and going of magnificence and pomp, through the coming and passing of man from darkness into darkness.

The weird, inscrutable stone of destiny.

It lay here in the abbey amid the silences of the past. Amid the splendid, magical ghost pageants of the London that was gone. Amid the tombs of those who had grasped the sceptre.

A great, dull stone.

The immenseness of the tumult of the Town was around the abbey. But it heeded it not.

It waited in silence with its dead. A wondrous a place holding within it the quietude of a strange invincibility. Its statues lay in the dimness. The voice of the light spoke softly in its glorious windows. Epochs came, epochs were gone. Kings came, kings passed.

It waited as on guard amid the tumult and the roar of the Town. Arch, pillar, roof, nave and transept were held in a ghost stillness. Day followed day, year followed year, epoch followed epoch. Ever there was a coming and going.

But the abbey waited with its dead.

I AM NO BELIEVER IN CIVILIZATION, but if it were possible for me to believe in civilization, I would certainly believe in the old Greek civilization.

For I am swept out of myself by their consonant and balanced expression of the beautiful as I look upon it here in the Museum. I am thrilled as I stand before their pictures carven in the lasting stone. And could I rid myself of the feeling that human slavery ought not to exist, I would wish that I were one of those old, glorious Greeks.

The Greeks stood upon the bodies of slaves even as do we, the men of the present time. But let us be fair to them. At least they were just and generous enough to feed their slaves.

And how are we to know but that there was some fine and wonderful thing in the mode of their lives, the knowledge of which their writers and artists have been unable to pass to us? It is not given to the greatest men of genius to fully picture the times in which they live. And even were genius dowered with this supreme picturing power, it is surely not to be thought that it could pass the full light through thousands of years to another race.

It is not for us, the descendants of the old Norse pirates, to have any adequate conception of the light that shone in Greece. We can but stand before the fragments of their glorious art and wonder.

Woven stone. It is as if the artists of Greece were able by a magical power to weave stone. There are times when their effects are as light and subtle as the effect of a leaf moving in the wind. Their marble draperies look as if they would yield to the touch. These artists knew the secret of evoking in stone the effect of delicacy and subtlety and movement.

This wondrous art of Greece! This glorious expression of a wise people who realized that the things most worth having in the world were beauty and joy.

As you stand and look upon their pictures in the lasting stone you feel that the sunshine was in their lives. You feel a sense of uplifting even when the subject is sad. For all the effects are sane and healthful and balanced.

These Greeks were a people who lived round and full lives. Their philosophy grew out of the contemplation of the beautiful things that lay around them—that they saw around them. For the world has in it a beauty unimaginable despite the cliques of ruling fiends who so often spoil it.

And so it was that the sublime Greeks did not look for guidance in dim and misty ideals. They were materialists in the sense that they took the apple of life as it was offered them. They had the wisdom to realize that a beautiful thing is not evil just because it is beautiful—that wisdom that is so rare in this English land of sadness.

From the Greek materialism sprang a life of wonder and glory.

I care not for the Romans. Nor am I in any way impressed by the accounts of their conquering wars. They were essentially a brutal, arrogant, domineering, inartistic people.

Administrators? Yes, they were administrators. But administration is exactly the thing that makes the world unfit to live in. It is the administrators who cause wars, it is the administrators who cause revolutions. The world is sick unto death of the insolent men and the insolent nations who have the assurance to lay down the laws for other men and other nations.

Administrators of necessity become corrupt. The Romans had a genius for the bossing of other people. They interfered with everything and everybody.

In a word they are responsible for the present, anarchic, social slave-state that is called civilization. They are responsible for the perpetuation of the idea that it is well either to enslave or be enslaved.

Their faces are hard and terrible. And cold and calculating. They look as men who had absolutely no sense of the rights of other men.

It is as if the whole history of Rome were told in the terrible faces here in the Museum. These men slew and crushed wherever wind blew and water dashed. They went out into the world making slaves. They were absolutely the most merciless people in history. And despite what any modern slave may say, their predominance, and the influence of their predominance, was and is against the developing of the idea of human liberty.

I am pleased to think that in the end the fine Goths smashed and humiliated them. But the evil was already done. The influence of this arrogant, domineering people had gone abroad.

It is hard to think that the fine Greeks were vanquished by the Romans. The people of intellect and joy and art were forced aside by people whose ideals were mathematical and pushful.

I suppose it is a dreadful thing to say, but to be quite frank I am in no way taken with the face of the great Cæsar. It seems to me to be but the face of a very acute, remorseless, pushful man who would sacrifice absolutely anything to gain his ends. I know that history falls and adores Cæsar. But I care nothing for that—I go but by the face that I see before me here in the Museum. He gained a great reputation by the conquering of comparatively unarmed peoples with a highly effective and disciplined army.

There are people in the world who say that a thing or a reputation that is hallowed by time ought not to be questioned. That even if it be questioned the reputation is so great and the questioner is so small that it does not matter. But it does matter. Men who endeavor to be free must question what they choose to question. They must be browbeaten by nothing. They must face all things.

How curious and powerful is the face of Hadrian.

It is a face the meaning of which I can neither grasp nor understand. And the face of Nero. Was Nero so abnormal and destructive as history makes him out to be? His face is as the face of one who had vast and bestial appetites, but at the same time there is in it a look of nobility and loftiness. It is undoubtedly the face of a man of large ideas. A face at once Olympian and bestial.

I feel that in some way history is not fair to this strange and terrible emperor of old Rome. For a man's character lies open in his face. It is there to be read.

This terrible Roman emperor! What was he really like? What was the side of his character that he showed not to the outer world?

Who is to tell?

These old pictures in marble that are here in the Museum. They are as lights shining from out the far past.

As you go through this place, that tells of the past, it may be that there will come to you thoughts of the profound differences lying between the races of men. For the Museum is the world's human document. It tells of the coming and going of men. Of the rising and falling and passing of lines of strange kings. Of man's ambitions and strugglings and fightings. It tells of things mysterious and significant.

But for me the most significant thing of which it tells is the profound difference lying between races.

Man has not solved the mystery of man. Science has but delved and fumbled and made loose assertion with a positive air. We know nothing real of the beginning of man. Indeed, the only thing real that we know is that in the beginning there existed mighty and potent races. It is as if we looked through a profound reach of time and saw a dense mist, and as if that dense mist suddenly rose and disclosed some strange race wondrous and puissant. And this is the only thing real that the egotistic thing called learning has to show us.

My feeling is this: This world is but a stopping place to which come beings from worlds separated by distances illimitable. For a while they stay and then they pass through a void immeasurable to other worlds.

For the soul of man is immortal, despite what may be said to the contrary by people of science. The soul of man passes on a stupendous journey from world to world. Now staying in worlds dark and dreary. Now living in worlds of unimaginable brilliance.

Man believes in a life after death. And is one to give up this beautiful and wonderful belief because of a few modern delvers who have the assurance to say that they can gauge infinite mysteries by their puny resolvents and little mathematical laws. Away with these small men who are called the men of science! It would be more to the point did they do the labor of real men in the fields. I have no belief in them.

I feel that the mysterious phenomenon called race is the sign that marks souls bound on a certain journey. The Greeks were neither as the Egyptians, nor as the Arabs, nor as the men of Africa. And so it is today. We, the white men of the West, are not as the men who are black, nor are we as the yellow men of the East.

May it not be that different races of men had their genesis in different worlds? May it not be that their souls began their world-to-world pilgrimage from places set immeasurably apart in the heavens?

There are worlds and worlds lying behind even what man calls the farthest star. Worlds, shining, illimitable and wondrous.

And as I wandered along through the Museum I thought of the futility of attempting to bridge over the profound and mysterious differences of race.

For me the Egyptians are the most wonderful of all the people of antiquity.

The picture-concept that comes to my mind as I pass by their strange gods and their statues in the Museum is that of a people mighty and wise and calm. A people possessed of weird powers and secrets. Surely these people, of the time gone thousands of years, held within their grasp the subtle powers that are called the powers of magic. They must have known of the power lying behind life. A people skilled in the reading of omens and the weaving of enchantments.

How great and weird and terrible are their gods! From what far world of strangeness did these Egyptians journey from in the beginning? Was it from some world of immense and dreadful powers and shapes? Some world in the Beyond of unimaginable strangeness.

Their dread, strange-shaped gods appall me.

Who is to tell of all that these mighty and wise people knew? Did they know of the secret of passing through the air, or of the striking dead by a wave of the hand? Or could they pass themselves at will through a solid mass? Did they know of the secret lying behind fire?

How strange are their faces. At once wise and benign and awesome and sinister.

I feel that these Egyptians knew of the way to control the mystery of the life-force. They knew of the secret of the arresting of decay. But they stayed not, but passed. For their life in this world was but a small phase in their stupendous, illimitable journey.

These people of the calm, wise, indomitable faces! Here in this world they lived in a land of light and sun. A land wherein lived a wonderful river.

Thousands of years have come and gone and we behold them through the reach of time, a potent, strange people. We know not of the time of their coming.

A people of mystery and tremendous, dread gods.

AN-KHEFT-KA. He lived in the time of the Fourth Dynasty, nearly six thousand years ago. He was one of the royal race.

A terrible life is in his face. And he stands in a threatening attitude.

It is as if he suddenly came to stillness whilst the blood pulsed fierce and vivid within him. As if he willed it that he should stand through time to show what manner of men lived long ago in Egypt.

This statue is as if it lived. The fire of life, and the vividness and potency of the fire of life, are arrested and held within it. It is even as if one of magic power suddenly arrested a flame as it shot fiercely to its highest—and as if the flame stayed as it was through thousands of years.

The face of this man of old Egypt is sinister and dread. A face of sudden destruction.

It is as if he held within him the deathpower of myriads of men. As if with a blow he might destroy a multitude. As if his very thought would kill and wither.

A face human and not human. The very power of destruction within it is not as the power of destruction known to us—the men of this present time.

This An-kheft-ka might kill from afar. He might project from himself subtle and dreadful forces of death.

The face of this Egyptian brings fear as one looks upon it in this strange room.

And before the vision appear the people of old Egypt.

They appear in the silence with their gods. One sees them through the profound Afar in strange, clear pictures. Their vast, shining towns appear. Yonder arise the pyramids.

The radiance of the sun falls shining upon their wonderful Nile. These people of the past. Whither have they gone? To what far world have they carried their magic and their wisdom and their secrets?

And strange thoughts come to the mind as one stands here in the great room in the midst of the signs and tokens of these people of the long, long ago. One thinks of the coming and the going of men. Of the passing, and the mysterious journeyings of races. Of the silence that falls.

And one is filled with hope.

For the silence of death is but the sign of the reaching of a stage upon a profound journey.

3

The Birds.

THE SONGS OF THE BIRDS come forth with the beautiful soft summer dawn, and the air of the opening day is thrilled with joyful sounds.

Clear, ringing sounds that seem far away as the stars that have faded off in the gathering light and that still seem near. Surrounding, beautiful songs of birds in the English dawn. Glorious, thrilling, swelling, heavenly songs, bidding joy into the coming day. Myriad songs joining into one great, mighty song. The offering of the birds to the coming sun.

These magical, ethereal bird-voices, rising at the dawn of the day and swelling forth in the clearing heavens! Voices beautiful as the light itself.

I arise and listen, and am carried away to some realm of wonder and strangeness, some far, far realm, mayhap, behind even the stars that are now gone. Would that I could tell of the thoughts and the feelings that come to me as I listen to the songs of the birds in the dawn! But they are not as the thoughts and feelings that come to the mind as one goes forth with men in the heat of the day.

It may be that as I listen to these voices I am at one with the whole of the world's myriad and wonderful life. For I feel the strangest exaltation and power and knowledge. It is as if these voices were telling me the very secret of life itself. These myriad, beautiful voices with their multiplex songs sounding as one illimitable song.

This sound, glorious and magical.

It is as if it upholds the world. As if it were of the very essence of life itself. Glorious and mighty bird-song, serene and strange and full of mystery! What may you mean?

I listen in wonder as the song goes forth.

And here is the life of the day in its fullness.

And the song falls.

I WATCH THE BIRDS AS THEY FLY through the air. I watch the strange flight of the swallow. Its flight is at once easy and swift as a flash—a gliding, curious, floating motion. It is as if it barely makes effort with its wings, and still it moves so swiftly in odd curves that the eye at times can scarcely follow it.

To me the swallow has the strangest flight of all the birds. A flight vague, elusive, oddly curving, unsteady, with a strange effect of floating and still with a lightning swiftness. Here-there-around-gone-here again—as if floating—darting swift as a flash. I marvel at the flight of the swallow.

Birds there are that fly as if they were breasting waves. Their flight has not the ease and strangeness of the flight of the swallow. The swallow is a thing of the very air itself. A thing to which the secret motions of the air are revealed.

And, again, there are birds that move in the air as moves a swift, powerful swimmer in steady water. These birds propel themselves with even, strong, rhythmical strokes of wing. They rise and fall slightly in their moving as a swimmer would rise and fall. It is as if for them flight were a thing of science and calculation. As if they were things not of the air, but things that had mastered the air.

There are birds that appear to fly with a steady, unvarying motion. As air-mariners going straight to a destination. Following some mysterious line.

And birds that fly up so high that the eyes can scarce see them. How strange it must be to be up so far over the world!

And birds that fly proudly and grandly and calmly. Such as the splendid eagle. I have watched the majestic, sailing, wondrous flight of the eagle as I have stood down in the pass of some lone mountain chain. This solitary king of the illimitable air ocean. Sailing proudly and calmly. At times motionless.

It is strange to watch the eagle sailing high in the still solitude.

FLYING FEATHERED HOSTS GOING FORTH on long journeys over land and sea. Going along over invisible air roads, avoiding the sweep of mighty storms, journeying to their destination with mysterious prescience!

How wondrous are these air hosts. These flying legions, dowered with that secret, inner wisdom that we who are earth-chained call instinct! How strange it is to see them pass. High up they go along over their invisible roads. Over the land, over the sea, over plains and mountains, over wide rivers, across valleys and fertile places. Magical hosts, passing high in the light of the sun. Who would not wish to be at one with them? How wonderful to shake off the earth-chains. How wonderful to pass swiftly in their midst. To see the world unroll. How magical to go with the feathered hosts along the invisible air roads.

I am thrilled as I watch them flying up in the far blue. And the thought comes to me that it is surely not we, the earth-chained, who own the world. Rather is it these flying feathered peoples. For them is the world in all its magic and beauty and glory. For them is freedom. For them is dominion. These fine and magical people of the air. These glorious people of the strong wings. I am thrilled as I watch them.

THERE ARE TIMES IN DREAMS when I feel that I have broken the earth-chains, even as they have been broken by the magical feathered hosts. I, too, have dominion over the illimitable air ocean. I can ascend into the air at will. I can pass over high mountains and over immense chasms. I can pass over seas. But the motion is not as a flying motion. Rather is it that by some power within me, that is no physical power, I can ascend and pass without effort through space.

But only in dreams. And still, who is to know the reason of dreams? May not the memory of a past, gone by unaccountable æons, arise in dreams? Who shall tell? Who shall know? May there not have been a time when man had dominion over the air? If not in this world, then in some world far, far away. For the feeling comes to me at times that we have lived in other worlds. And that we will live in other worlds. May not dreams be at times memories, or mysterious prescience of a future? I feel that they often are.

And it comes to me that a man could not feel that he of himself had dominion over the air were there not some reason for it, secret and profound. The dream life is surely life, even as the waking life is life.

In dreams I feel that I have broken the earth-chains. That I have dominion over the air. And the memory of the dream is with me as I see the feathered hosts passing in the afar air.

THE FLYING FEATHERED HOSTS HAVE laws as we have laws. They have their ruling dominant ones, and they have among them those that are far-seeing and wise. They have language and habits and customs and codes. They have a philosophy that is not as the philosophy of us who toil and strive here below. They know things that it is not given to us to know.

These fine and magical people of the air.

How wonderful they are. How strange and thrilling are their morning voices. Often I think of them.

These offerers of song to the dawn.

4

The Coming Of Romance.

A S I SAT TO REST under the great tree, after going along
the road, it came to me that there were times when our England
was the most beautiful place in the whole world. Above me the sky
was blue and clear and strange. The air was soft and warm, and still
without languor. And around me rang the voices of the birds. And
soon I could make out the deeper and stranger voices of the earth
dwellers in the wood behind.

A beautiful day. A day such as you might not meet in the whole
of the world save in this, our England. And in the blue above there
passed a faint, strangely-shaping cloud.

And the spell of the romance of England came over me. This old,
storied land. This place of beautiful green grasses and wood and
water and hills and gently winding rivers. Away in far places I had
thought of its charm and softness, and had longed to see it again.
The vision of its beauty had come as I had gone over arid, wide
plains. I had been thrilled by the romance of it from afar. And now
I was with it, was of it, I was held within the spell of it on this soft,
beautiful summer day.

T HE SOUND OF A BELL came through the air. And a picture of the old Norman times arose before me. The times when the bells rang at the close of day to impose quietude. And was it that I heard shouts? And the shock of battle? Did I see dark, quick, moving masses of men? And fallen men with faces torn with pain?

Here under this great tree, on this beautiful summer day, clear pictures set in a cloud-vagueness appeared before me. The pomp and magnificence and splendor of the courts of old! And strange-sailed ships going out to far adventure! And scenes historic! Yonder sat John Lackland[32], signing the Charter! And yonder was the gay and blithe Robin Hood who robbed robbers! And monks and abbots and gallants! There was Cromwell of the face of iron! Clear, passing pictures.

The Romans! They came as if through the air. Compact legions of helmeted men with shields and short swords. The driving, resistless, world-conquering legions of the old, living mighty Rome. I heard the low rumbling of the wheels of chariots. And there came scenes wild and strange! Of men living in the deeps of forests. Of crouching, wild-faced men with peering eyes. Beings who dwelt forever in the midst of dread. The crouching men of the Beginning.

The England of the past! Of story, of fable, of tradition, of romance, of deeds dark and dread, of splendor and magnificence and chivalry, of jousting and tournament, of kings and knights and squires, of strong men-at-arms. This England where grew men.

And was its romance gone? Surely not. It lived here in this beautiful summer day. It was in the very air. England had not changed. There had been but a passing of men. Men had come and men had gone,

---

32 "John Lackland" was a nickname of King John of England (1199–1216), signer of the Magna Carta. So called because as a younger son, he was not due to inherit significant lands from his father, King Henry II.

epochs had come and epochs had gone, there had been a passing of lines of kings, there had been wars and the dying down of wars, and the passing of parliaments. A revolving of events. But this summer day was surely as the summer day of centuries gone. This tree under which I sat was a tree of the old, far time. It had stood through the passing of generations. And the bell that was now sounding through the soft warm air! Might it not be that it had sounded out in the far-gone times even as it was sounding now!

The wind stirred through the great tree. And I looked up above to the blue that appeared through the green leaves. As seen through the leaves there was an effect in the blue of mystery. And on the edges of the leaves was a golden shining. Green and mysterious blue, and golden shining. And the golden sound of a bell in the air. And the clear pictures that were rising and passing before me.

A thralling, surpassing, enchanting effect. As of a picture in which the past and the present were mingling.

I AM ROMANCE," SAID THE SHINING FIGURE. "I guard the things that live in what man calls the past. And I bring them before the eyes of those that see. There is no present, there is no past. There is no death. There is but life that comes and comes again. Men die not, they but change.

"I am a wondrous story. I inspire the hearts of men. I am the giver of eternal youth. I am behind the things of wonder and beauty. I reveal to man the glory and the power of himself.

"There are times when I live in strange places. There are times when I reveal myself strangely. I impel men to go forth into the unknown.

"I it was who lit the wonder of the world to man. And where I dwell not neither is there light nor beauty. Neither is there hope. There is but darkness.

"I am the light shining in the distance. I am the light shining from out the past. The change that is called death visits me not. I am now as I was when man first beheld me."

How strangely sounded the voice here in the soft air that had now become stilled. A voice that came forth with a thrilling, silver clearness and that still had in it a deepness.

In the air was a strangeness. It was as if all things had become hushed at the sound of the voice. I could no longer hear the bell.

"Behold!" said the shining figure. And lo! there came before me a picture of exquisite and glorious beauty. I saw a green and wondrous land in the midst of which were cities shining and magical. Wondrous cities of wide gardened spaces. Fountains glistened high in the air. And the air above the cities was of the clearest and purest blue. The beauty of nature. And the beauty of the places arising from the hands of man were wedded together.

A vast and splendid picture of moving and passing life, and still a picture of which I could see the whole. A clear, luminous picture of transcendent beauty.

Music and joyful sounds filled the air. And now I could see clearly the people of this glorious land. Never had I even dreamed of women so fair, or men so brave of look.

"This is the land of England that is to come," said the voice of thrilling, silver clearness.

"But you are Romance!" I cried.

"I am Romance," said the voice, "but I am also Verity."

And the shining figure passed.

And here again were the golden sounds of the bell in the air. And the blue above was appearing through the green leaves.

I arose, and went along the road.

5

The Bridge.

HAVE YOU EVER LOOKED UPON a mighty bridge and tried to grasp the whole of its meaning? Have you ever tried to understand why it was that the columns of the arches beneath this bridge stood the endless pressing of the flowing river waters? Have you ever tried to fathom the reason of the beautiful curving arches remaining in their place?

Air and wind and water and frost and snow and storm and hail and rain are against this bridge. And still it stands calmly over the ever-moving waters of the great river. Generations have come and gone and still the mighty bridge is as it was. Firm and still and calm it stands.

For me a bridge is a more wonderful and beautiful thing than any work of art in any great gallery of the world. It is more beautiful and significant to me than the most beautiful picture of any great painter, I am more impressed by the majesty of a bridge than by the majesty of any vast work of statuary.

Day by day the people pass along upon it. They go and come and come and go. I tell you that this bridge is fuller of meaning than the most mighty and complex work of art. It has more to say than the greatest book. Its voice is silent—but if you stand and look upon it, to your mind will come its story.

A curious story.

In the Afar[33], dim profound[34], this great river flowed as it is flowing now to the sea. Man had not yet come into the world, but still this river was in being even as it is now. And lo! there came the men who were destined to bridge this river. Hundreds of thousands of years ago. Men came to the banks of the river and looked across the waters. And in the mind of one of them was born an idea. A dim, vague idea.

It was an idea wonderful as would be the idea in this present time of a ship of air sailing to a distant world. For to these men of the dim Beginning this river was a vague, affrighting, mysterious, insuperable barrier. In it dwelled dread and awful monsters. At times monstrous heads arose from it.

But to the mind of one of the men of the Beginning there came an idea at once vague and audacious and impossible.

It was then that this bridge was conceived.

HUNDREDS OF THOUSANDS OF YEARS ago, this bridge lived within the mind of a savage. Not as you see it now. It lived as a vague, distorted picture. It came to him in a flash, as he stood on the bank.

And he went away. And the time came for him to go to the earth from whence he came. And there was a coming and going of

---

33 Afar is the region and people in the Horn of Africa and part of the Rift Valley elevations. In Victorian-era writing, it symbolized the unknown and undiscovered.

34 "Dim profound" was commonly used in 19th-century literature to describe either a personal emotional or spiritual crisis or to represent a place of misery.

generations upon generations. But the idea lived on steadily, even as the river flowed. And there passed thousands of years. And the idea grew and grew.

And lo! the bridge was born!

It suffered. It was broken. It was swept away. The elements assailed it. Lightning shattered it. Storms smote it. But it grew and grew. It got stronger. It got mightier. It got subtler. It got wiser. It got to know the uncertain ways of the elements. It grasped the secret of withstanding the erosion of time.

And at last there came a day when it was even as it is now.

Firm and great, with massive, immense supports and beautiful sweeping arches. Could the man who dreamed of it, hundreds of thousands of years ago, come back to life and see it now he would be struck dumb with the wonder of this child of his imagination. For his dream was a dream vague and strange and impossible. He was not to know that as time passed, and men came and were gone, there would be those who would dream even as he dreamed, that his first idea was to grow in the minds of men to come and be woven magically and manifolded in myriad ways, till lo! in the end there was this mighty and wondrous bridge that withstood the eternal pressing of the ever-flowing waters of the river, that withstood the fury of the elements that withstood the snows and the hail and the rain—nay, that withstood even the very wear of Time itself.

Could the man of the dim Beginning come back to life he would prostrate himself and adore this massive and mighty and wondrous bridge.

I T IS NOT FOR YOU, as you look upon it, to grasp the whole of its meaning and its secrets. For it passed through the minds of countless men of the past. Slowly, slowly it grew. Men brought ideas to men. Ideas were woven and welded together. And variants of ideas were brought and added to the common store. It is not for you to grasp in its wholeness the magical realizing of the myriad ideas, and the variants of ideas, that are expressed in the one immense idea of this noble and mighty bridge. Enclosed in this one immense idea are ideas that took man tens of thousands of years to express.

This bridge is the work of myriads of minds extending through æons of time.

And so it is that you may not grasp the whole of its meaning.

It is not for you to picture the whole of it with utter clearness to yourself. It is not for you to grasp its inner secrets.

BOLD AND RESOLUTE MINDS ADDED their quota to the immense idea expressed in this mighty bridge. There was the one who conceived the daring idea that the supports of the bridge should rest down in the very bed of the mysterious river itself.

Men feared the depths of the river. For within the depths there lurked menace and horror. But there was among them the one who knew not fear. For a long time he thought of the bridge. He watched it swaying unstably in the moving waters. The swaying, unstable bridge was the beginning of the expression of the mighty idea. As yet it was at the mercy of the waters and the winds.

And there came to the one who watched the daring idea that was destined to express itself in the far time to come in a gigantic support of stone surely and deftly laid on stone. And when he gave forth his idea those who were with him were afraid, for to them the river was a being mysterious and terrible. They gazed with trembling upon the one who knew not fear. He would surely bring upon them destruction! They feared the anger of the mighty river. And there were among them those who spoke against him.

A ND SO IT WAS THAT this wondrous bridge was slowly builded through æons of time. It was passed from mind to mind. And man expressed the idea with his hands. And expression was woven from expression. Idea was builded upon idea. Men came, and men were gone. But the bridge grew even as a being of life and sentience. It defied and fought and withstood the elements. It passed from change to change. It attained to a stupendous might and power. It grew to be a thing of majesty and beauty and grace and might.

This noble and wondrous bridge!

6

Courage.

I T IS ALL VERY WELL to rail at the world because it erects its mightiest statues to men of courage. It is all very well to say that poets and philanthropists have more claim to honor than mere fighting men.

I believe in the beauty of poetry. I believe in the nobility of philanthropy. But the power of poetry and philanthropy never kept a destroying invader from ravaging a country and its homes. It never kept women and children safe.

The potent men in times of stress were men with firm faces and hard eyes, who shrank not from thoughts of blood and death, but went out and slew the approaching enemies. The dread, potent men of absolute physical courage! These were the men of value.

And the world rightly accorded to them higher honors than it accorded to other men, for the world, hard though it be, possesses a deeper and sounder wisdom than is dreamed of by the shallow, squeamish person who forgets that but for fighting men he would have no roof over his head.

The wisdom of the world is the mysterious and at times sinister wisdom of the crowd-mind which no individual thinker, however acute and profound, has ever fully grasped or ever will be able fully to grasp. For human beings, however near to each other, can never fully understand each other. Individuals are isolated fragments of an immense being that is wonderful and manifold and complex—the crowd-being. And this crowd-being acts on lines outside the comprehension of the wisest thinker. So sneer not at nor be impatient of the wisdom of the world—the crowd.

PERSONAL, PHYSICAL COURAGE IS THE only true and real courage. It appeals to all. All can understand it. The things that are called moral and intellectual courage are at best but things of comparison.

Physical courage is man's most glorious gift.

It is the power of absolute control of the body at times of imminent bodily danger. You are unexpectedly confronted with death, and lo! you are cool and calm. Your pulse beats evenly and regularly. Never have the powers of your body lived together with more consonance than now. Within your brain is a clearness. Nay, it is as if your brain were clearer and more collected than you have ever known it. Before you is the frightful face of Death. But within you is sanity and balance and collectedness.

This is physical courage.

And such is its magic that Death itself shrinks from you.

IT IS NOT ALWAYS GIVEN to you to know who is the man who is possessed of this wonderful courage-magic. And it may well be that though you possess it yourself you may not know of it. The circumstances in which you have lived have been such that you have not been put to the test. You have never known that within you lived this cold flame, magical and divine. You have lived out your life in an immense, noisome town. You have wandered not, nor have you mixed with the fine, hard spirits who live off in the far, outer world. You are pale, you are weak, you are one who effaces himself. You are one who knows not the smile of fortune. You are perhaps a submerged slave who lives down in the lowest deep of the tremendous town. An ill-fed, weakling slave.

And lo! you are suddenly put to the dread test. You—the one who is weak, the one who is nothing—are without warning faced with horrible danger. Your end is upon you.

And all at once there has arisen within you a force mighty and wondrous. A force that is at once cold and of fire. Your weak heart is nerved with an unknown power. A god has arisen within you. You are yourself a thousandfold. Your brain is alert. Your eye is acute. Into your face has come a strength—a fine radiance.

You, the weakling, are a force indomitable.

SOME THERE ARE WHO THINK that this magic of absolute and supreme courage may be acquired. But it is not so. It is born with the being who possesses it. And it is a quality of the soul that is not to be crushed out. Neither is it to be crushed out by the torture of the hell-life of the prison, nor by the grind and wear of circumstance. It is as a divine and eternal light.

True is it that you may be used and broken in to danger. You may work slowly out, unalarmed, along the yard when the storm is smashing and devouring the ship. You may stand steadily in the midst of hailing bullets. And still you may not possess this absolute and supreme courage.

Or you may be a duelist—one who has killed many men. Or a wholesale slayer of your kind.

This courage is to be known but by the sudden and unexpected test.

W HEN A COUNTRY IS IN danger this courage-magic is the thing that alone will avail. At such times the power of gold is as nothing if you have not men who are without fear. Neither do you want men of loud, patriotic words, nor the half-treacherous men of compromise.

Women have always loved the men of courage, for these were the men upon whom all depended. In the vague and dread time, gone by tense thousands of years, these men went forth and slew the immense and horrible monsters who were then the lords of the world. They went forth and faced tremendous and devouring dragons. They slew dread, giant tigers. And it was because of these rare men that in the fullness of time the human grasped the world.

These men of the courage-magic were the gods of the dim beginning. They went to the lairs of unspeakable brute forms and challenged them. They outfaced them in the depths of immense forests. And so it was that they were deified and adored. And rightly so. But for them some other being than man would now hold the world.

And they sailed forth in ships into the far, engulfing mystery of the ocean. These fine men of courage. They feared neither the sweeping waves nor the storms nor the dread monsters that rose out of the black depths to seize them as they stood on their heaving ships. They fronted blackness and mystery and death with indomitable faces. These men-gods of the old times.

They built nations and empires. Aloft they held the sword, and lo! beneath its protecting shade there sprung up the arts and the crafts and the sciences. The sword! Let us reverence the sword. For it brought into the world the magical calm of peace.

S O RAIL NOT BECAUSE THE world erects its finest and noblest statues to men of courage. And rail not at the sword. For from the sword comes life.

The world owes all it has to the men who were possessed of the magic of absolute courage. And the world will owe to them all that is yet to come to it. To these men, thinkers and statesmen and idealists are as nothing.

These men of the wondrous courage-magic are the men whose destiny it is to lead the world into safety and happiness. Away with your talkers and thinkers. Away with your men of compromise. The world is to be saved but by the sword.

These glorious men of courage! These descendants of the old gods! Let us give them homage and reverence!

7

The Zoo.

WHEN I GAZE UPON THE monkeys in the Zoo I am pleased indeed to think that there is a missing link. I am pleased to think that the purblind[35] know-alls of science have been unable to connect us with these unfinished and most objectionable animals.

Man is bad enough as he is. He is filled to the brim with what are called virtues and vices. He is not a particularly wise animal, but at least he is a fairly good-looking animal.

And so I feel it to be a thing most scandalous that the persons of science should be allowed to go on endeavoring to cast a slur upon his ancestry. True, they miss the casting of the slur by a link. And, as anyone knows, a miss is as good as a mile. But the endeavoring to cast the slur at all shows malicious intent, and in my humble view

---

35 "Purblind" is an obsolete word meaning partially blind or slow to understand. Peak usage was during the 1700s and remained common-ish until after World War II.

these persons of science ought to be locked up—or, at the very least, talked to with vigor and sternness.

Far be it from me to claim perfection for the race of beings to which I have the honor of belonging. Indeed, I will be frank enough to admit that in quite a number of ways we are not as intelligent as other races of animals. We like work, for example. Or—well, to be exact, some of us say that we like work. And there are other little faults of ours that I won't dwell upon because it might be considered not quite polite.

When I gaze upon the monkeys in the Zoo I feel that if it be really true that a handsome race like ourselves had such ill-favored ancestors it would be at the very least a graceful thing to hush the matter up—to say nothing about it. And all the books written upon the subject by the misguided idiots of science should be at once impounded and burned. And here I trust that I will not be thought to be a disrespectful ruffian lacking in proper reverence for ancestors. I do reverence ancestry, especially when it is hoary and ancient. But there is such a thing as looking too far back. And I think we ought all to be satisfied with dating our ancestry not farther back than Adam, who by all accounts was as handsome and as personable a man as the best of us.

I LIKE THE LIONS AND TIGERS in the Zoo. They look philosophical and well-mannered and contented, and as if they would eat from the hand. It may be that they yearn for the freedom of the forests, but if they do possess this yearning they certainly have the manners to hide it. How different is their style and behavior from that of our alleged ancestors! In fact, these same lions and tigers are the most benign looking animals in the whole Zoo. They gaze upon the throngs of people with the calm ease of monarchs. Animals at once gentle and dignified and indifferent.

Whilst I was in the Zoo a lion began to roar. He was a somewhat ancient lion with a large and gentle face and his roar had in it something of the quality of the foghorn and the voice of the ass. A tremulous, booming, resounding kind of a roar. Why he roared I don't know.

I have often read of the awfulness of a lion's roar. How that it was enough to freeze the blood with horror. But I must say that the song of the aged lion here in the Zoo had in it no sinister quality. Rather did there seem to be in it a quality of friendliness. And as he roared a sort of a smile came over his large and gentle face.

I might say here that I was once engaged in a lion hunt—with others. This hunt did not occur in the wide African plains. It occurred in the United States. The lion had escaped from a travelling circus to which I had the honor of being attached and my hunting implement was a modest pitchfork. The rest of the hunters were armed with sticks and whips, for our object was not to hurt the lion. Our object was to entice him home. We were afraid that he would suffer when he was out in the cold world on his own. And we were right. For when we found him sheltering under a hedge, he seemed to be quite lonesome and ashamed. He looked as if he were very sorry for himself. I suppose he was thinking of the dinner he had missed in his happy home in the circus. Anyhow, he followed his keeper back home with a gentle eagerness. And we—the hunters—followed the mild and amiable king of beasts with our sticks and pitchforks, and other big-game hunting implements, carried triumphantly over our shoulders.

I F YOU WANT TO SEE really ferocious animals in the Zoo you must not look for them especially amongst the Carnivora. Rather must you look for them amongst what might be called the vegetarians—the animals who indulge but in the eating of grass or vegetables. The buffalo, for example, looks as ferocious as a hundred tigers rolled up into one. And the rhinoceros looks pessimistic and vicious. Indeed, the vegetarian animals look generally as if they took somber and aggressive views of life. They have none of the mildness and benignness of aspect that distinguishes the lions and tigers.

The reason of this is too deep for me to fathom. And I will pass the problem by, save for the remark that the same thing seems to hold good amongst human beings. Vegetarians and teetotalers usually are— But I will pass on, lest I give offence.

The wolves in the Zoo are restless and energetic animals, who look almost as vicious and as pessimistic as if they subsisted solely upon vegetables. Forever they are pacing hurriedly the floors of their cages. Animals lacking philosophy.

They have a bad reputation. But I can't help thinking that they are not quite as black as they are painted, for when I was in the Hartz Mountains I came across tame wolves in the streets of Goslar. They had been got when cubs, and they had grown up and become domesticated in the houses of those that kept them just exactly as would dogs.

In fact, I was very much taken with the idea of bringing a wolf cub home to England and rearing it up.

Physically the wolf is a perfect and beautiful animal. It is built at once for speed and strength and staying power. A balanced, wonderful being—the result of thousands upon thousands of years of hunting.

HOW MYSTERIOUS ARE THE ELEPHANTS! They stand, strange-formed and gigantic and tremendous and massive. Beings of an old, old race. Looking as if they had come from some world of their own.

Immense, stumbling beings of shapes suggesting a sinister world of gloom and darkness. Misshapen giants with weird and wonderful eyes. How wise and strange they look! Were they at one time the dominant beings of the world? Did they strangely reign in the midst of beings dread and amorphous?

These wondrous things with the eyes of mystery! They come from out the past dim and profound. From out a world where lived beings, dreadful and appalling and gigantic.

And surely must it be that they reigned over the world long, long before man came to it!

Bart Kennedy

On Work and
Not Working

Lou Ambers tips his hat as he accepts a sandwich from a hand
reaching out of a doorway, 1935

1

Concerning Work.

I T IS SAID THAT THE world will be saved through work. But I fail to see it.

Indeed, a blind man might see that this ideal of work is mainly put forth by acute people, who live fatly upon the labor of those who are more or less unintelligent. And I am sorry to be forced to record the fact that these acute people have often been backed up by those whom the world alleges to be profound thinkers.

I like Carlyle[36]. His prose weakens one up. But I wish he had not had this bee in his bonnet concerning toil.

---

36   Thomas Carlyle (December 4, 1795 – February 5, 1881) was a British histo-
rian, satirical writer, essayist, translator, philosopher, mathematician, and
teacher. His work included *On Heroes, Hero-Worship, and The Heroic in
History*, where he argued that the actions of the "Great Man" play a key role
in history, claiming that "the history of the world is but the biography of great
men." His major works include *The French Revolution*, 3 vol. (1837), and *On
Heroes, Hero-Worship, and the Heroic in History* (1841).

    A great polemicist, Carlyle coined the term "the dismal science" for
economics. He also wrote articles for the *Edinburgh Encyclopaedia*. Once a
Christian, Carlyle lost his faith while attending the University of Edinburgh,
later adopting a form of deism.

Man has done a good deal of work in the world, and how is he the better for it? Is he happier? He is not. Has he as good a time as the animals? No.

However, it is only fair to say that no really intelligent man works if he can get out of it. He becomes either a statesman, or a thinker, or an artist, or an overseer of the labor of others. The nearest approach that a really intelligent man gets to work is to make other people do it.

By nature I am a most sympathetic person, but I must confess that I cannot summon up sympathy for the man who says he is fatigued through the effort of making other people work. The profound fatigue of the statesman, or the thinker, or the overseer moves me but little. Whenever I hear of it, I wink the other eye. For where is the man who is too lazy to be a thinker, or an overseer, or a statesman? Show me the tramp who would be too lazy to join the Cabinet! Why, I wouldn't mind joining it myself!

And here I must let you into a secret concerning the mental make-up of the tramp. He is not the cynic the world supposes. There is someone for whom he has a reverence and a regard. There is someone to whom he looks up. In his heart of hearts he has a hero.

This hero is the politician who has attained his ideal of drawing a stout and handsome salary for the good of his country.

True, the tramp realizes that all politicians are job chasers. However noble and lofty and ideal the politician might be, he still keeps his weather eye upon the possibility of doing work that is at once light and dignified and exceedingly well paid. And the nobler and purer and loftier the politician is, the more he is anxious to get into a position where he can guide his beloved country—which is but natural and patriotic.

In mathematics, he is known for the Carlyle circle, a method used in quadratic equations and for developing ruler-and-compass constructions of regular polygons.

The tramp knows all of this desire for work on the part of the politician. But he forgives it. For it is work that he would not mind doing himself.

Whenever I go to Westminster I am struck with the resemblance that exists between politicians and tramps. To the unseeing eye there is, of course, a difference, but this difference is merely one of apparel. Both tramps and Parliamentarians have the same expression of eye. Both wear the look of introspection that comes to those whose work lies within the realm of thought.

Especially the statesmen who sit on the Front Bench[37]!

I, an old tramp, am filled with admiration and reverence as I gaze upon them. Had I been a cleverer and more intelligent man, I would have attained to the privilege of sitting amongst them. But I do not feel jealous. For how can an old tramp feel jealous of men who are skillful enough to earn big salaries in the way they earn them? Their work in life is to sit easily and think, and when they are tired of thinking to get up and say what they want to say, and then to sit down again. It is grand. These statesmen have attained to the very summit of the tramp's ideal—they loaf and lounge and talk, and they are paid handsomely for this loafing and lounging and talking by a grateful nation.

Splendid!

It only proves this: that the world, in reality, pays homage to the tramp's ideal, which is to abhor the doing of the thing that is useful.

I must dispel here an illusion that some people have to the effect that the tramp is a danger to the State. Never was there illusion more baseless.

---

37 "Front Bench": In many parliaments and other similar assemblies, seating is typically arranged in banks or rows, with each political party or caucus grouped together. The spokespeople for each group will often sit at the front of their group, and are then known as being on the frontbench (or front bench) and are described as frontbenchers. Those sitting behind them are known as backbenchers. Independent and minority parties sit to the side or on benches between the two sides, and are referred to as crossbenchers.

The tramp is too much of a philosopher to be a revolutionist. As long as he can live without the doing of useful work, he is as satisfied with life as the most brilliant Cabinet Minister that ever slept in Westminster.

Neither is he a Socialist. For the Socialists are parlous, unimaginative ruffians, whose ideal it would be to make everyone work—even to brilliant Cabinet Ministers!

Neither is the tramp a Liberal.

He is a Conservative to the backbone: a conserver of his energy. And should the Liberal statesman be hypocritical enough to bring in any repressive measures against him, I hope the Conservative statesman will remember the tramp's politics, and annul these measures when next their turn comes to receive stout salaries for lounging upon the Front Bench.

THE TRAMP LOVES THE OPEN air. When I was drawing my parallel between the statesman and the tramp, I ought to have mentioned that if there be a crumpled roseleaf in the statesman's downy bed—taking it from the tramp's point of view—it is the fact that the statesman has to earn his salary by lounging and thinking in the inner air. The tramp would hardly like this. However, if he were a statesman, he might console himself with thoughts of the nearness of the Terrace[38] and the long and joyous holidays!

The open air!

---

38 The Terrace Pavilion of Westminster Palace, meeting space of House of Commons and House of Lords (London)—A 265-foot promenade along the Thames river once popular for tea breaks and informal meetings for members of Parliament. Since 2014, the Terrace can be rented by the public for seminars, soirées, and weddings.

Is there anything so grand and fine and beautiful as the open air? How glorious it is to go along to no place in particular, neither thinking of nor caring for the morrow! Despite what fools—who are sometimes called wise men—may say, man gets more out of life when he lets tomorrow take care of itself. I never was so happy in all my life as I was in the old days of wandering along. Security! Man, when he is in a healthy state, cares absolutely nothing for it. Security is at best but a cowardly word. I know men who are "secure." I know men who have plenty of money. And, taking it all round, they don't get as much out of life as those who live from hand to mouth.

To walk along in the glorious sunshine. How wonderful it is! How bracing it is to go along in the keen and healthful cold! To work one's way through the storm! It brings to the body power and strength. There is beauty even in the fall of rain.

How wonderful is the open air!

The fine glamour of the unexpected!

It shines into the life of the tramp. As he goes along he wonders what will turn up next. He is faced with the mystery of the changing, inscrutable face of life. Life holds for him an interest that it holds for no one else.

Yes, he begs his bread! And what of that? Who is to despise him because of that? Surely not the one who lives off the labor of others! Surely not those who sit in the governing chambers of the world! These men of parliaments, whose mouths are filled with glowing and noble words! Surely it is not for such as these to say that the tramp is one who is lacking in dignity!

L ET ME SAY THIS IN SERIOUSNESS.
It is not that I believe labor with the hands to be inherently base and ignoble. The world itself has it that labor with the hands

is a degradation. A man who labors is a man who is ill-treated and despised. I care not what lies may be put forth by well-paid parasites. The one who labors is the one who is degraded.

I know what I am talking of, for I was one who labored. For years I worked, and my lot was lower than a dog.

And so I became a tramp, and in becoming a tramp I became more of a man.

Again, I do not say that there is no such thing as intellectual labor. There is. But I hold that the most real labor of all is labor with the hands.

All men should labor with the hands.

This is the way that the tramp looks at the question.

He is the one who is born into the slave class. He is of the vast, dark pit that lies at the base of the social fabric. He is of the strange, dreadful world that lies far underground, a world of darkness hideous and terrible.

He must work with the hands so that he may live. But so hard, so terrible, so merciless is the task that is set him that he rebels against it. That is, he rebels against it if he has inherited any spark of manhood.

And so the one who is a slave goes forth into the world. He goes forth into the light and the shine of the sun. He refuses to work longer. Better it is for him to beg for his bread than to endure slavery down in the darkness.

He possesses not the craft nor the power nor the opportunity to live off his fellow men. He goes forth, one who is homeless and nameless. Life for him is hard, but he no longer dwells underground. There comes to him a strange philosophy. There comes to him the wisdom that comes to those who wander in isolation.

Those who labor not, but who live in high places, say that he will not work. True, he will not work. Not one of the laws that can be devised by well-fed governmental drones will force him to work. The tramp has realized that even death is a finer thing than slavery.

He has become wise.

As he goes along the road, things that have been long obscure to him become clear. He sees that the world is overflowing with people who are trying to get out of the doing of labor with the hands. The world is filled to the brim with shirkers. No one wants to work. Not even the dullest slaves are satisfied with it. They would all get out of it if they could.

He sees the hypocrisy of the shirkers who are cute enough to live well without the doing of real work. He appraises at its true value their indignation concerning himself. But he is philosopher enough not to blame them too much, for he knows that if all men took life as he takes it, the cute drones would have to work for their bread. He understands their anxiety. He understands the anxiety of Members of Parliament, and all the loafers of the official class.

So he takes things easy. For he has at the very least as much right to live as anyone else.

Hardship! He doesn't mind it. He becomes healthy and contented.

He sees the truth that the world has gone foolish on the idea of rush. It is made plain to him that animals are certainly wiser than men, though they may not be so clever.

He knows that trouble will come to this civilization, but not from men like him. It will come from the idiot slaves whose ideal is to be as well off as their masters. He has as little use for Socialists as he has for Liberals or Tories.

His ideal is to be free, and at the same time do no work.

He is the only honest shirker of work in the world. He is the pioneer of a finer and calmer life.

He wanders along, a real philosopher.

2

The Value Of A Book.

In my long tramp through the mountains in the north-east of Spain I found a book that I carried in my knapsack to be of great value. It procured me attention and respect and a desire to fall in with my wishes. It was better than a hundred passports. Everyone bowed before it: arrieros, propietarios of posadas and ventorros, guardia civiles, and all the priests and great señors of the little mountain places. It was indeed a magical book. It gave me status and position. Whenever I got into a difficulty I produced it and all was well. The propietario bowed, the priest shook me by the hand, and the great señor of the little place became affable.

It fed me when I was hungry, did this book. For often I would get to a posada (inn) at night and there would be practically nothing to eat. The man or woman of the posada was sorry, but there was nothing for me but wine and a little bread. They were sorry, but it could not be helped. There were no huevos (eggs), no meat of any kind, no vegetables, hardly any salt. In fact, there were none of the appetizing things that make a meal a meal. And sometimes they were not even sorry that this state of famine existed. The patrons of the posada were mule drivers who carried their own provisions and who slept on the ground at night. The luxurious traveller had not as yet corrupted the worthy innkeepers of these mountains. They were plain, honest, natural folk who were living now as they had lived five hundred years ago. And they expected the casual wanderer to have gumption enough to carry his own provisions.

I would listen to the story of famine, smiling to myself all the time. And then I would produce my magical book. And a change would come over the posada. Everybody at once took the kindliest interest in me. I was asked questions that I had not the slightest hope of understanding. Eggs and meat and vegetables and bread were quickly set before me. And the loafers of the posada thronged around me as I attacked the viands, watching me with the deepest interest and respect. They made a multitude of remarks about me.

The children were brought in to look at me as I was devouring the provisions. I was experiencing that most gratifying sensation—the actual blossoming of a common, ordinary nobody into an admired and respected somebody. I was changing, so to speak, before my own eyes. At first I had not even excited curiosity. And now I was exciting deep and respectful admiration. And all through the book. I had not thought very much of the value of books up to the present.

In fact, I had been rather doubtful as to whether they possessed any real value at all or not. But now my mental attitude was changed. I would never say a word against books again, for here was I enjoying a fine meal, accompanied with the most soothing kind of respect, on the strength of one. And as I watched the Spaniards from out the corner of my eye passing this book reverently around, I began to think well of the world. I had been feeling pessimistic as I tramped hungrily through the mountains. But now all was well. All through a book.

When the book was reverentially handed back to me, I beamed on the crowd and conversation began to flow. I had, of course, in the meantime been given the best seat near the fire. And I drank the wine of the country and listened to the talk and talked myself. I need hardly say that I had no idea of what the conversation was about. All that I knew was that they were talking about the libro (book). And they had no idea of what I was talking about either. But the Spaniards are a polite race.

This magical book was a book that I had written myself. It was the first time that it had been of any real value to me. The Barabbas who published it had thought very little of it. At least his appreciation of it had taken but slight tangible form. But now even I began to feel some reverence for it. It had turned out to be worth its salt. It provided me both with food and respect. It made me a personage in a lonesome and strange country. It made me a man that it was well for people to know. A person to be sought after. And as I drank the red wine of the country and took my ease before the fire in the posada, I began to realize that being an author was not such a bad thing after all. At least it was not such a bad thing here in Spain. In England an author was usually only a dubious person who could not pay his debts. But here in Spain it was altogether different. And as I sat before the fire I began to see the virtues of Spain in a most rosy light.

Of course none of these people could read English. In fact, hardly any of them could even read Spanish. They had as yet been unspoiled by education. But it was here that my publisher had come to the rescue. When he had published the book he had insisted on making my portrait the frontispiece. The Spaniards could not read print, but they could read a picture. I, this very man who was sitting drinking wine before the fire, was the one who had written this.

There was my picture in front libro (book) of it!

They had never seen an author before, and they probably would never see one again. Now was their chance. And I was pointed out with pride to all the people who came into the posada. I was requested again and again to show the libro. It was opened by the newcomer and I was again compared with the picture. It was a strange, glad and comforting experience.

The point as to whether I was a good, bad or indifferent author never entered their heads. I was an escritor (author) and that was enough. I was a sort of comrade-in-arms of the great Cervantes. My talent they took for granted. I was one to whom respect had to be shown.

I was travelling through the part of the country where the great Miguel de Cervantes had lived centuries before. Though the people could not read, they still had the greatest respect for the art of letters. And this respect took the practical form of receiving with open arms a passing tramp who chanced to have his picture in a book that he had written. I was given the best place by the fire, and the best part of the floor of the posada to lie on during the night—the part farthest off from the great door.

At many of the posadas they refused the money I offered them for the accommodation I had received. They considered the honor of entertaining an escritor as sufficient payment.

At last I got to Alcalá de Henares, the place where the great Miguel Cervantes was born. It was a big, walled town, and my knapsack was examined by the guards outside the wall to see if there were anything taxable in it. At first the guard was inclined to be stiff with me. He glanced at me with suspicion as he began to examine my knapsack. But the moment he came across the book with my picture in it all was changed. He called for the other guards to come and look at the distinguished stranger who was honoring the birthplace of the great Cervantes with a visit. At the time I was ignorant of the fact that Cervantes had been born in the town. But the guard soon made me understand. And I was treated with the utmost respect and honor. My rough-looking, trampish appearance was ignored. I was a distinguished stranger. An honor that had descended upon the town.

The guards escorted me with great ceremony into Alcalá de Henares. In fact, the outside gate was left to take care of itself.

They brought me to the best fonda (hotel) in the town, and they left me in charge of the propietario after explaining at the fullest length who and what I was. And then they saluted me, and I saluted them. It was one of the proud moments of my life.

And thus it was that this book with my picture in it turned out to be a good thing for me in my long tramp through the wild mountains of the north-east of Spain. It smoothed away the difficulties from out of my path. It was better than a hundred passports. Everyone bowed before me.

These people of the mountains were kind and helpful towards me just because I had written a book.

3

A Sailor's Life.

I HAVE OFTEN WONDERED WHO the poet was who sang of the free and beautiful life that the sailor is alleged to enjoy. I mean the romance-of-the sea and the free-bounding-billow poet. I have often puzzled as to where he got his information concerning the joyfulness and the idealism of the life of good old jolly Jack.

Upon what ship did this poet sail?

Alas! I fear that he sailed but in a beautiful ship of his own glowing imagination. Where else could he have got his free bounding billows and his romance and his good old jolly Jacks?

Billows to be sure are free, but if you are on the foredeck in the winter-time in the Western Ocean you will find that they are also cold, and you will wish that they were not quite so free. And as for the romance of the sea, well, it would require something more than the imagination of a poet to perceive it after you had enjoyed the gaiety of forecastle life for a month.

It may have been that this poet was of the days of old—that he was a pirate. If that be so, he naturally saw the life in its most vivid and colorful aspect.

I have never been a pirate, so I don't know. I mean I have never had the happiness of being a real, brass-bound, well-fitted-out, gory pirate. I have, to be sure, been an oyster pirate. But that doesn't count. You are then but a thief in the employ of respectable, honest, God-fearing fishermen. You are not on your own. And, as everyone knows, stealing for others is a most unromantic business.

The truth of the matter is that a sailor's life is, to put it mildly and quietly, a somewhat Spartan life. In fact you might say that it is a somewhat rude life. It is a life from which dreaming idealism is largely excluded. Indeed, I don't think I am going too far when I say that a sailor of a dreaming and ideal turn of mind would not have to sail long before he was wakened up by the butt-end of someone's fist.

And here I beg leave to state, parenthetically, that there is as much knocking about of sailors now on the high seas as there ever was. Of course there are consuls! There are, God save the mark! There are. But be a sailor, and go and make a complaint to one of them. And then you will get to know a thing or two about consuls. And if you should ever have the happiness, gentle reader, of becoming a sailor, and you get knocked about, take my advice and don't go to a consul when you get ashore. For he has a chilly and cool way of looking at these little things. Besides, you are wasting the gentleman's valuable and precious time. No—your best plan is to meet the mate ashore!

I was once aboard a boat where there was a mate who had a fancy for knocking men about. I am not going into any details. I will just content myself by saying that I was left alone, the reason being that the mate knew that I would kill him if he struck me.

If you are a sailor and you wish to preserve your personal dignity you must be a man of the positive order.

Parliament takes an interest in the sailor. But it is an interest only of a certain character. For in Parliament there are too many men who have an interest in jerry-built and badly-run ships. However, I am not going to abuse Parliament. For it does the very best it can—for itself.

The fact is that the sailor's life is the hardest life going. And to be quite fair I must say that the real reason of its being the life it is, is because of the surrounding conditions. The monotony and the iron celibacy of the life make men harsh and evil-tempered. And the men in command become tyrannical and cruel.

I knocked about in ships, off and on, for about three years. I had, of course, the roughest end of the life—being in the forecastle. But in my view the life aft is pretty much as bad as the life forrad[39]. The people aft get better food and they have an easier time, but the general conditions are the same.

The whole of it is a dog's life.

I MUST CONFESS, HOWEVER, THAT MY sympathies are with the men in the forecastle. For they are always treated worse than they need be treated. And whenever I hear of a mutiny I am against the people aft. For I know. I know that the people aft must have goaded the sailors beyond human endurance. I know that the people aft must have got even less than they deserved. For to mutiny aboard a ship is a harder thing than to mutiny even in a prison. A mate may strike you, and if you strike him back he may shoot you like a dog. Your only chance is to kill him if he strikes you. If you don't, you will get small consolation from the consul ashore. For consuls are always against the sailor man. They are either bribed, or they are against a sailor man instinctively.

People who have not been sailors may look upon these words as hard words. But should any sailor man read them he will know that they are true words—absolutely true as Gospel.

---

39 "Forrad" is Scots dialect for "forward" and was primarily used by sailors until the middle of the 19th century.

I have seen men struck. I have seen men treated with indignity. Interfere? Why, you couldn't interfere. It was almost more than the best man's work to look out for himself.

Cruel and cowardly things are done at this present time to men at sea.

AND THE GREED AND CUPIDITY of the ship-owners are largely to blame for this state of affairs. They put pressure on the captains to make the ship earn more money than it can earn. And so the ships are made too hot to hold the men, so that they will desert at far out ports and their wages be saved. This mean trick is being carried on at this present day. I care not who the lying ship-owner is who gets up in Parliament and denies it.

And the captains are expected to drive the men, and to cheat them out of their proper allowance of food.

All to make money.

In one way I am as sorry for the captains of ships as I am for the men.

It would be a good deed to Shanghai a few ship-owners out of Parliament and ship them for a hundred-and-fifty-day trip aboard a good old lime-juicer.

Here is a fact: In the last twenty years the comfort and luxury of the saloon passengers has been catered for tremendously. In fact, a saloon passenger may voyage over the ocean in an immeasurably more comfortable and luxurious way now than was possible in the old days. And I might further add that the comfort of the other passengers has been very much increased.

Competition has forced the ship-owners to do their best by the passengers. To travel the ocean now is a dream.

Things have advanced for everybody.

For everybody but the crew. The firemen and sailors now are as they were twenty years ago. Great ships are designed now for the comfort of everybody.

For everybody but the crew.

A few months ago I went into the forecastle of a crack liner as she was crossing the Atlantic.

It was as the forecastle of twenty years ago. The crew had still to pig together. They had to sleep and eat in the same dark, ugly, narrow forecastle.

The ship-owners are without souls. It is useless to say anything to them. But the public ought to be let know the fact that the better the crew is treated the safer is it to make these perilous ocean journeys. For even though you have the finest suite imaginable aboard a crack liner, you are still dependent upon the crew to carry you in safety to your destination.

The crew who still live in the dark, ugly, narrow forecastles of the days of old!

The better they are treated, the better they then can do their work. And the safer you are.

4

On Living Long.

EVERYBODY IS TELLING EVERYBODY ELSE how to keep fit and well and live to be a hundred. And as I know as much, or rather as little, about the subject as the next man, it seems to me that it is high time that I got in and made a remark or two.

I have never been ill in my life. But why I have never been ill is a mystery too deep for me to understand. Perhaps the real solution to the mystery is the fact that I have always been well. And I think that this is about as near as anyone gets to the matter, even though the sage be a titled doctor with the whole of the unfortunate alphabet straggling after his name.

You are ill because you are ill; you are well because you are well. You live to be a hundred for the simple reason that you have never been thoughtless enough to let yourself die. You die before forty because you didn't live.

To the casual person this way of putting it may appear bald. If it is so, I am sorry. But it is all the real knowledge I have been able to extract from the specifics that have been put forth by the wise and great doctors concerning the various ways to live happily and merrily for a hundred years.

In my view, a good way never to be ill is never to go to a doctor. For it is, of course, part of the doctor's trade to see danger looming ahead. The poor man must make a living.

If you don't go to a doctor, you very likely won't know you are ill. And that is something. Indeed it is more than something. It is pretty nearly it all.

I like doctors. They are good fellows to meet when you are well. But I can't help thinking that a man knows more about his own body than the most skillful doctor that ever took a big fee. Of course, if you break your arm or your leg somebody must pull it straight. Perhaps there is something in surgery, though by all accounts the surgeons are but too curious about seeing the body's inner works. One would have thought that there were enough unfortunate people in hospitals for them to practice upon. But such is evidently not the case. A surgeon—especially if he be distinguished—is usually a seeker after knowledge with the knife.

It has taken the human body millions of years to evolve from a simple life-form to its present state. And I hope I won't be thought too much of a cynic if I doubt the ability of any man to know anything real concerning the way it works. And added to the subtlety of the structure and the working of the body, it is affected in an infinitely complex way by differences of climate, and habits, and food, and age, and a hundred other things.

Away with you, gentlemen! Away with your drugs and your knives and your wise and sympathetic expressions! You know far less than the old Indian medicine men! Why? Because your knives have given you a little knowledge—which, as the poet aptly remarks, is a dangerous thing.

S OME PROFESSORS OF THE ART of living happily and merrily and long say that we eat too much. Some say that we drink too much. Some say that we ought to be teetotal, that we ought not to smoke. Some swear by good old wine—which I think is sensible, if you can get the wine. Others believe in exercise. Others in rest. Others in plenty of hard work—an opinion with which I beg to differ, the reason being that the healthiest men I have ever known were tramps: gentlemen who were much in the open air, and who did as little as possible.

As to eating too much, well, I agree that it may be bad. But it is not quite so bad as eating too little, despite what may be said by the food philosophers. If you don't believe me try it. Be in a position where you have not the money to buy sufficient food and you will soon find out eating too little is hardly the golden panacea it is alleged to be.

Eating rich food is also wrong. Well, try eating poor food. Try the difference between crossing the Atlantic in the steerage and the first cabin. And come and tell me how you felt after each method of crossing. I much fear that you will vote for the first cabin every time. I have tried each method and I know which I would vote for.

There is a good deal of nonsense put forth about the value of plain and simple food as against the value of rich and varied food. And there is a good deal of nonsense talked about eating too much. It is difficult to eat too much, if you are really fit and well. And the best food for you is not necessarily the plain and simple food that the food philosopher recommends. The best food for you is the food you like best. And in ninety-nine cases out of a hundred the proper amount for you to eat is the amount you wish to eat. And never forget that when you are eating it is not the food philosopher who is eating. It is you!

As for being teetotal, well, I hardly know what to say further than to remark that teetotalers are usually very poor advertisements of their theory of life. Try and think of a lifelong teetotaler who looks anything of a man. You may to be sure know several. But I, personally, have never had the good fortune to meet them. The teetotalers I have met have invariably been weeny-looking, crabby, skimped-up, miserable, dead-and-alive persons. It's a pity that the temperance people don't take a leaf out of the book of the hair-restorer people. I mean it's a pity they don't hire a few fine-looking, moderate-drinking men for exhibition purposes.

Some believe in the taking of all kinds of weird exercises. Personally, I don't go much on weird exercises. The animals don't seem to indulge in them, and the animals are at least as healthy as we are. And the finest-looking men I ever saw were not takers of set exercises.

I believe in plenty of easy walking in the open air. But I don't call that exercise. I call it pleasure—sheer, unadulterated pleasure.

I know that I am absolutely certain to live to be a hundred—if I don't die in the meantime. And this is as much as the wisest prophet can say.

If I might be allowed to hazard a suggestion to you as to the way to keep fit and to live long, I would advise you to get some person to leave you five hundred a year. You could then go into the country and take it easy.

Taking it easy! Ah, the idea has come to me at last. Take it easy! Don't be bothering your poor head about whether you will live short or long. Eat as much as you want, and eat the best you can get. Don't be always wondering as to whether you are well or ill. Give doctors the widest of wide berths. They are a good lot of fellows, and I suppose have the right to live. But they know too much for the ordinary, plain man. Or rather, I mean they know too little. When you are ill, the best thing they can do for you is to look wise and let your body cure itself. If your body can't do this, you will die. And I am sure you will agree with me that you can die without the doctor's assistance.

Here is my recipe:

Take things and life easy. Eat what you like, drink what you like. You will know yourself, better than anyone can tell you, when things don't agree with you. And go on and on till you can go no more.

5

Exercise.

THE VALUE OF EXERCISE IS that it brings about the condition of struggle under which the human body was evolved.

It has taken man some hundreds of thousands of years to attain to his present lofty position of general lord and bottle-washer-in-chief of this universe. Some hundreds of thousands of years ago he had not quite all the say. In fact, he had to sing somewhat small, for the great flying reptiles with the unpronounceable names looked upon him as mere provender.

And so it was that man had to do a bit of dodging about. For his friends the reptiles were nearly as rapacious as the modern American trusts. They ate him on sight, and I may say that there were other beings—also with names not to be pronounced—who had the same liking for man's most intimate society.

In a word, our friend man has had a humorously interesting time right from the beginning. He has always had to dodge and hustle and fight and scheme for a living.

And so it is that we, the heirs of everything in sight on this planet, are born dodgers and hustlers and fighters and schemers. Every organ and every sense that belongs to us is the fruit of continual stress and struggle.

Rest is a most beautiful and satisfying thing, and I am very fond of it.

But too much rest is not good for the body. I am sorry to have to say this, for I have the deepest respect for rest. But the sad fact is that when you indulge too much in rest you are going against the foundational principle upon which your body was built.

I know it is sad, I know it is hard after a man has stolen his pile by the way of trade not to be able to rest and take it easy. But he can't. He must keep on doing something or another. If he doesn't the clock will stop.

I HAVE OFTEN WONDERED WHAT REALLY is the best exercise for a man to take. I know, of course, there are dumbbells and Indian clubs, and muscle-developers of every variety and shade. I know that there are systems whereby pale and slight persons may—in their own room—develop powerful and fear-impelling proportions. But I believe not in these things.

And here let me put forth a commonplace that any trainer knows. There is such a thing as normal strength, I mean the strength that properly belongs to you when you are in health. By a certain course of training it is quite easy to make a man stronger than he is normally. This is usually done when a man is being trained for a prize-fight. You get your man up to a certain point of physical power and you make him fight at that point. But remember this: There is always the tendency for your man to sink back to his normal point of strength. And the trainer has to study and time this tendency with the greatest care. For if your man begins to sink to his normal strength you get the condition of lassitude that is known as being stale.

What I am driving at is that you can only force your strength at the expense of your vitality. No man can properly appreciate the delicacy and the subtlety of the human organism. And that is why it is well to be very careful.

The truth of the matter is that the soundest and fittest people are those who take exercise on lines that are as near as possible in accord with the lines upon which the human body was developed from the beginning. Man did not learn to dodge the great flying reptiles by the use of dumbbells and Indian clubs and scientific muscle-developers. He learned to use his eyes and his ears and his feet and his hands. And perhaps it is well to record the fact here that the tiger owes none of his grace and swiftness and power to the use of puerile, artificial, over-advertised devices.

The soundest and fittest men I have ever met were not athletic in the exact professional sense. They were men who worked at different kinds of work in the open air. Men who had done all sorts of work—but always in the open air.

The open air! That is the whole secret. Man really belongs to the open air.

Absolutely the best exercise of all would be to go and earn your living in the open air.

HUNTING IS A FINE EXERCISE. But in these days no one can hunt but those who have people to work for them while they are hunting. It is a grand thing to be shooting pheasants all day in the open air. But this is only within reach of the class who live upon the fruits of the slavery of others.

Hunting big game! This, when the condition is that you must get your living by it, is coming pretty near the exercise indulged in by your woad-stained ancestors. It will sharpen your wits and keep bright the powers of your body.

The exercise that the brigand indulges in must be truly delightful. Here he is, in the fine, clear open air, waiting for the good Samaritan to come along with his capacious and well-lined purse. True, the Samaritan may turn somewhat crusty, but what matters that? There is always a crumpled roseleaf in the downiest bed.

And here I must confess that I am always sympathetic with the ambition of the budding youth who is fired with the idea of going off to be a brigand. Alas! he is nearer the good, honest, normal, primal man than he is ever likely to be again.

Empire building! That is another glorious exercise. And once a friend of mine paid me a great compliment. This friend told me that I ought to be out doing the rough work of empire. I seemed to be the right type of man.

Yes, it would be right enough. But the humorous part of the idea is that it is the stay-at-home, patriotic, doesn't-know-one-end-of-a-gun-from-the-other tradesperson who invariably collars the swag.

The unfortunate empire builder gets the kicks and the glory.

But I must not digress, I must pass on to the more exact consideration of my subject.

Walking is a fine exercise. It is within the reach of all. Never take a cab or a bus and you will save your health as well as your pocket.

Yes, walking is a good exercise—but fighting is a better. To go on a campaign is to renew your life—that is, if you don't lose the number of your mess. It is a glorious thing never to know what is coming next. And the food you eat on a campaign does you a great deal of good—when you get it. Go out on the next campaign, my boys!

Going on tramp is also a fine exercise. The beautiful wide country road where— but, I believe, I have said this somewhere before.

I will wind up by confessing that this exercise business is somewhat of a mystery to me. There are people who know exactly what everyone should do to become a cross between an Antinous and a Hercules, but here let me remark that those knowledgeable people make a living out of their interesting information.

I have endeavored but to give forth a hint or two. My hints may be valueless but believe me when I assure you that if they are, they share this quality with hints in general upon this elusive subject.

6

Success.

S UCCESS IS BY NO MEANS the greatest test of talent. The man who wins the race is not always the swiftest man, nor does it always follow that the battle is won by the best fighter.

I have known so many good and sound and clever men who have gone under, and I have seen so many bluffers and fakers come up on top, that I am forced to the conclusion that success is mainly born of qualities that are not the best in a man's character. You may be as talented as you please, but if you lack push and brag and bounce you will find yourself in a poor way. You must be ready with the quick and skillful lie at the psychological moment, you must be an adept in the fine art of double dealing, and, above all, you must have the faculty of explaining how wonderfully clever you are to other people.

I have watched the game through the whole of my life. I watched it when I was a laboring man. And even then, when my head was somewhat thicker than it is now, I noticed that the finest and the best men were never picked out for promotion. Rather was it the ready and swift and cute liar. Indeed, I have watched the thing that is called success through the whole of my vivid and varied career.

And I think I can afford to say a word or two about the matter, for I am not a soured failure. I have achieved success myself.

You may think, my reader, that my labeling myself as a success is neither diffident nor modest. You are right. And let me tell you that if you are to become a success, you must leave diffidence and modesty very far behind indeed.

My ambition was never to make money. My ambition was to become known, and to live without injuring myself with rude toil.

To be successful is to do what you want to do in the world. And being a monied nobody would not have suited my book.

Making money is no test at all of success. It only means that you have been able to steal without the vulgar necessity of having to go to jail. I know plenty of men who have made money. And the greater part of them are but poor specimens.

And whenever I read the thrilling confessions in the Press of how men began with sixpence and ended by stealing millions, I am saddened by the lack of humor displayed by the average millionaire. Instead of burdening a tired world with badly put platitudes, he ought to tell us how he managed to keep out of jail.

His copy would then be worth printing.

Pickpockets and burglars, and confidence-men, and sand-baggers, are simply gentlemen whose souls are lit up with the millionaire ambition. And it is with sorrow that I see them gracing the dock. For there are millionaires who are not at all bad fellows. Their main fault—if they have one—is that they possess not an able-bodied sense of humor. They seem to be saddened by the thought that the world is full of dishonest ruffians who have designs upon their stolen millions.

They are not philosophers.

R EAL SUCCESS HAS SOMETIMES a good effect upon a man's character. For, curious to relate, there are some decent fellows who have been successful. If you are a decent fellow, people won't be so apt to be jealous because you have beaten them in the race. And if you have fairness enough and humor enough not to be continually making it out that you are successful simply because of your transcendent talent, the world will be grateful. For the world knows as well as you know in your heart that it wasn't altogether your talent that did the trick. The fact of your being a shrewd, smart, unscrupulous fellow helped you immensely. But for your ability to handle people, you would still have been an unrecognized genius. You were able to please people. You were able to make people feel how wise, and clever, and noble they were. And so you got your chance.

All this the world knows. For the world is wiser and shrewder than the wisest and shrewdest man. It has lived longer. And it, therefore, likes you to take your success easily. It likes you not to put on airs about it. It likes you to be courteous enough to realize that very likely cleverer men than you have never achieved success.

If you act fairly about your success, the world will be pleased and grateful.

And here let me break a lance on behalf of worldly people. I so often hear them run down by noble and lofty and good and pure people, that occasionally I feel vexed.

Worldly people are often blamed for going on the other side of the street when they see the woeful and broken-down failure coming slowly along. And noble philanthropists often call these worldly people snobs and cads. But the reason that people go on the other side of the street when they see the abject failure coming along, is not really because they are snobs and cads. It is rather because the abject failure has upon them the effect of cold water being poured down their backs. They are afraid of him. Just as they would be afraid of anything cold or wet or miserable. I am not talking now of the man who is merely unsuccessful. I am talking of the abject failure.

Worldly people like a successful man who is a good sort very much indeed. For there comes from such a man a stimulation. It is good to know him, to see him, to shake hands with him. His success has made his personality bigger and broader. There is something in his eye and in his smile that is likable. He is a man of sense and fairness. A good, jolly, fine, generous fellow. And he is all the better, and is liked all the better, because he looks the reason why he gained success straight in the face.

A successful man who is stuck-up and unpleasant about his success is really half a failure. People perhaps kowtow, or have to kowtow to him, but in reality they hate the sight of him. For he is one who is not fair and honest. He does not play the game. He is that worst liar of all—the liar by implication. His manner implies that he is a big and wonderful person, who honors the world just because he lives in it. He has the discourtesy to be forever making people feel that he has beaten them in the race. He knows how he won the race, but he is not honest enough to own it.

For such a successful person I have the most utter contempt. Yes, I have it, even though he were a man of genius.

So if you are that rare person, a successful man, take it easy. Don't go along without noticing people. If a man wants to talk to you, let him. And try to realize that you are not altogether successful because of your lofty and commanding talents. Try to realize that you would be nowhere did you not possess sharpness and cuteness. Try to realize that were you an exactly scrupulous and honest man, you would never be where you are. You had to master the art of blowing hot and cold.

You owe a great deal to the devious side of your character. Had you been a finer and a better and a more honest man, you would have failed.

So don't give yourself airs. Don't be stuck-up.

7

Doing Nothing.

I DON'T KNOW WHO IT WAS that brought the idea into the world that doing nothing was an evil and wicked thing, but whoever he was he was an enemy of universal human joy and enjoyment. For to my unregenerate mind there is no such soothing employment—if I may be allowed the use of an Irish bull[40]—as doing nothing in the midst of pleasant surroundings.

---

40 An "Irish bull" is a ludicrous, incongruent or logically absurd statement, generally unrecognized as such by its author. The inclusion of the epithet *Irish* is a late addition.

  The "Irish bull" is to the sense of a statement what the dangling participle is to the syntax, or, in other words, a jarring or amusing absurdity is created by hastiness or lack of attention to speech or writing. Although, strictly speaking, Irish bulls are so structured grammatically as to be logically meaningless, their actual effect upon listeners is usually to give vivid illustrations to obvious truths.

  The Irish bull can be a potent form of self-conscious equivocation and satire in the hands of a wit's sharp tongue. As such, it is associated particularly with new or marginalized populations, such as the Irish in Britain in the 19th century, or the Jews and Germans in America in the early 20th century.

I know that it is said that those who do nothing get excessively bored after a time. But I fear that I must take this saying with at least a large grain of skepticism, for if the people who do nothing are so awfully bored, how is it that we so very rarely hear of them taking a refuge from this boredom in the doing of work? There must surely be more charm in the doing of nothing than meets the eye of the stern moralist.

I know, of course, that insects work—some of them. Bees and ants revel in the delights of industry. But whoever heard of any of the higher order of animals working, unless they were forced by man. You will at once mention the beaver, I know. But he is the exception that proves the rule. And I must say that the fact of his working so hard makes me unable to join in the general chorus of praise for his sagacity.

Really noble and self-respecting animals do nothing, and delight in the doing of it. Some of them hunt, but you can hardly call that work, for even the most pronounced doer of nothing be he of the man breed—will hunt.

The fact remains that all self-respecting animals do nothing when not interfered with. They are not skilled in book philosophy, but they have brains enough to know that the sun was given to them to bask in, and that the world generally is not half such a bad place if you will only take it as it is and not be forever trying to displace things and trying to get hold of a knowledge that in the end means less than nothing. These animals have not the privilege of possessing human souls, but they have souls enough of their own to be above the doing of work. Of course they have not the intelligence to work, you say. True they have not. And I might add that they are not particularly ambitious to possess such intelligence.

I am a man who is egotistical, but I am not egotistical enough to think that we human beings know it all. The longer I live the more I am inclined to doubt the all-magic of the human mind. Believe me when I assure you that the other animals know a thing or two that we don't know. They neither write books nor build motor-cars, nor do they make foolish guesses about the planetary system. But they know enough to let one another alone as much as possible—a thing that we with all our alleged wisdom have yet to learn. And they know other things that neither you nor I nor any other man know anything about.

They are wise enough to know that to live is in itself the highest and most absolute thing of all. They are wise enough to know that if they do this they do everything.

BUT I APOLOGIZE. This is getting serious. And besides it is going away from the subject. We were talking about doing nothing.

The world suffers from misdirected energy.

I would have you all gay. I would have you all taking your ease.

Let us be frank. You know as well as I know that your secret ambition is to do nothing. Out with it. Isn't this a fact?

You may, of course, be that rarest of rare birds—the man who loves work for work's sake. If you are this man, then all I can say is that I am not addressing you. I am talking to those who like loafing—those who are like myself.

And let me tell you a secret. I am really lost in admiration for the people who live well and who at the same time do nothing. The exquisite wins my deepest respect.

But there are people whom I respect even more than the exquisite. I respect—as I said in the beginning of this book—statesmen and politicians, and I respect artists. So lost am I in admiration of these people that I would willingly subscribe for the building of a statue to any one of them. Their art is the art of arts. And I am pleased to be able to say that the world thinks as I think, for the world erects statues to as many of these people as come under its notice.

The world is full of faults, but it knows a thing or two after all.

It realizes that this thing called work is not quite the grand and unutterably beautiful thing that the foxy philosopher or the stern-browed alleged thinker says it is. I often say hard things against the world, but even I must admit that it has a sense of humor. Its humor is a humor that has a bite in it, but better this humor than none at all. And the world knows that what I am saying about the doing of nothing is quite true. And I shouldn't wonder if I, myself, were rewarded with a statue in the fullness of time.

THE OUEVRE OF BART KENNEDY

Darab's Wine Cup, and Other Tales, Etc. (1897)

The Wandering Romanoff (1898)

A Man Adrift (1899)

London in Shadow (1902)

A Sailor Tramp (1902)

In a Tramp Camp (1902)

Stone Fishing (1902)

A Tramp in Spain (1904)

Slavery (1905)

The Green Sphinx (1905)

Wander Pictures (1906)

The German Danger (1907)

A Tramp's Philosophy (1908)

The Hunger Line (1908)

The Vicissitudes of Flynn (1909)

The Human Compass (1912)

Soldiers of Labour (1917)

The Voice in the Light: Tales of Life and Imagination (1917)

Thought-Coin (1921)

Brain-Waves (1923)

Golden Green (1926)

Footlights (1928)

Founder and proprietor of *Bart's Broadsheet* (a weekly started in 1921)